BUILDING MANAGEMENT BY PROFESSIONALS

by

Ray Moxley

Butterworth Architecture
An imprint of Butterworth-Heinemann Ltd
Linacre House, Jordan Hill, Oxford OX2 8DP

 PART OF REED INTERNATIONAL BOOKS

OXFORD   LONDON   BOSTON
MUNICH   NEW DELHI   SINGAPORE   SYDNEY
TOKYO   TORONTO   WELLINGTON

First published 1993

British Library Cataloguing in Publication Data
Moxley, Ray
  Building Management by Professionals
  I. Title
  690.068

ISBN 0 7506 0443 3

Library of Congress Cataloguing in Publication Data
Moxley, Ray.
  Building management by professionals/by
  Ray Moxley.
      p. cm.
      Includes bibliographical references and index.
      ISBN 0 7506 0443 3
      1. Construction industry – Management.   I. Title.
  TH438.M63   1993
  690'.068 – dc20   92–2429
                                                                        CIP

Disclaimer
It is inevitable that there will be errors and changes in
information and procedures set out in this book at the time of
compilation. No two contracts are the same. Neither the
author nor the publishers can accept responsibility for loss or
damage resulting from this material.

Printed and bound in Great Britain

Contents

Preface

The building industry is now aware that it is used by governments as a regulator whose capital supply can be restricted when the economy overheats. This has happened every seven years or so since the war. It devastates the training of craftsmen, managers and professionals. A large proportion of the unemployed at such times are members of the building industry. Highly trained and experienced people leave for good. When building recovers, it overheats more quickly. The stresses on each part of the industry either reverse or change. Recession decreases workload, increases competitiveness, improves quality and services and bankrupts good firms. Boom does the reverse.

If ever equilibrium is achieved and maintained, reasonable value for money may result without the devastation.

This book addresses the problems the industry faces in better times.

As the principles behind good building management apply to all the participants, they are repeated to some extent, but from the viewpoint of each discipline.

Acknowledgements

I would like to thank Michael Armstrong, a friend, client and author of many books on management; Robert Heller for his wise words on 'motivation'; Geoffrey Trickey of the QS firm Davis Langdon and Everest; Michael Davis, a friend and deputy chairman of the services contractors Drake and Scull; Nigel Thompson of Arups and Andrew Boulton of Fairclough the contractors for the many hours of valuable discussion drawn on much varied experience in the formation of the Design-Construction Group thesis. For the inspirational experience of excellent facilitative project management I must thank 'CC' Smith, who created a positive approach in the fast-track building of Chelsea Harbour. He was part of the Lehrer-McGovern team headed by Fritz Rehkopf. John Anderson, director of P & O Group, and Ron Davie have provided invaluable direct experience of really tough site management and organization on large contracts. Patrick Emett, my old QS friend, now a partner of Wrightson Pitt & Emett, works closely with me still on large and small works. I appreciate his positive and fresh approach and thank him for his work included herein. Finally I would like to thank my co-directors and partners Ann Scampton and Paul Hains for their hands-on AMM/DPC experience and support.

1

Introduction

The British building industry, compared with most western countries, is inefficient, expensive and slow. It turns in inconsistent standards of quality and has a complex structure. The standard form of contract (JCT) used on the majority of building work is considered by some to be unfair to the client. One eminent legal authority said that the architect who recommends it renders himself liable to an action for professional negligence. Official reports point to the ill health of our building industry, for example the report by Slough Estates comparing British performance with other countries, or Walter Weiss's comparison of German and British building organization published in *The Society for the Advancement of Methods of Management Newsletter* No. 5.

The changed nature of contracting

Many British architects and engineers are good at producing design, production drawings and details. They are not perhaps quite so comprehensive in their work as their American colleagues, and only a few of them undertake the quantity surveying role and give building economics advice, as do their German colleagues. But their role has been diminished to the extent that they are, for all practical purposes, excluded from the

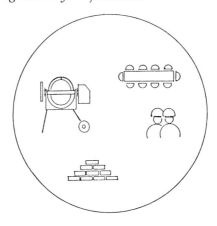

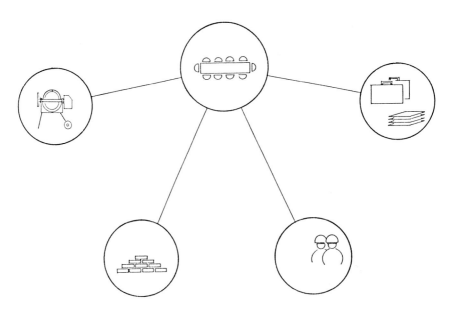

Figure 1.1 *Changes in contracting organization from single companies containing several departments (top) to holding companies with separate specialist limited companies of trade contractors (bottom).*

direction of the work on site. This 'Ivory Tower' position is slowly emasculating their practical knowledge of construction, and in the long term may reduce their role even further. This will be bad for the whole industry. For good design and its sensible interpretation is what has made British architecture so renowned in the past and still pulls many visitors to historic buildings each year. Good design is producing a renaissance in German architecture, with good quality right through to the smallest detail.

The designers' decisions affect every aspect of the materials, the components and their assembly. To save money on design is to prejudice the consistency of the whole job and is an obvious false economy.

Not only are the clients unhappy about the state of the building industry, but the professions are seriously worried, for instance, by the claims for extras that accompany the progress of most tendered contracts. The Building Research Establishment has noted that the average overrun of Crown contracts (until recently almost half the total building industry's output) is an average 30%, which means an extra cost on contracts of about 19% and this on 'fixed price' contracts. Architects no longer control the trade contractors who employ the craftsmen who actually make and assemble buildings. As a result, programmes are difficult to enforce, and quality is variable.

The builders are dissatisfied with the situation. The good ones dislike having to use the claims mechanism in order to survive. They are irritated by the architects' decreasing lack of practical understanding. The trade contractors, themselves, dislike their dependence upon main contractors who can hold them to ransom over payments for work completed and being, often, prevented from feeding in their knowledge and experience back to the designer.

The quantity surveyors watch the situation and are at a loss to recommend measures which deal fundamentally with the situation. Their frustration causes them to look towards project management, though design and detailing are not part of their training.

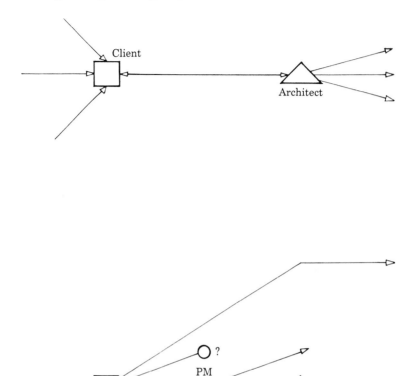

Figure 1.2 *Direct communication between client and architect/design team (top) can be interrupted by the independent project manager (bottom).*

Focus on activity

The key to the ills of the building industry lie with the design team first in the office and then on the site. This is 'where it all happens' and it is possible to manage the contract in such a way that most, if not all, the ills so far mentioned can be eliminated. The reward is good cost control, consistent quality, much improved speed and a reliable programme. The total all-up cost is not significantly different and there are no big claims for extras. Most of the procedures to be recommended in this book can be applied in groups. But taken together they make a radical change to the whole process which is a considerable improvement upon orthodox methods.

Sampling site activity

Site meetings

Someone experienced in the matter of building knows that in a short space of time a fair picture can be obtained of what is happening on any particular site. The regular site meeting will indicate a number of vital things about the following:

1 The competence of the people around the table.
2 The compatibility of those present one with another.
3 Who has positive attitudes wanting to complete the building efficiently. Who is obstructive and thinking negatively.
4 The information coming from the consultants: are the materials and methods proposed of the right quality and appropriate to their function? Or are there faults in the flow of information?
5 Is a claims file being built up by the contractor?
6 Does the site agent have control of the programme? Do the participants understand the relationship of the activities shown in the programme.
7 Is there involvement of the sub-contractors with the professional team at the meeting or are these people kept out of sight?
8 Is the client disturbing the logical process of the works by unreasonable requests for amendments, or is the builder using requests for amendments as a reason for claims and delay?
9 What are the attitudes of the various consultants?
The architect and the assistant architects.
The structural engineer.
The services engineer.
10 Communications: is the chain complicated and bureaucratic or is it simple and effective?

Site condition

An inspection of the site will provide a useful impression. Depending upon the stage of the work, the following things should be noticed:

1 Security fence: is it secure and is there a hoarding against any part which abuts the public pavement? Is it kept in decent repair?
2 Storage of unfixed materials: are the bricks and blocks etc., stacked in a well organized way? Are they protected from the weather? Are they amongst muddy ruts or can they be approached cleanly from a hard surface?
3 Unfixed components: are windows, doors, sanitary goods, etc. stored out of sight and secure in a proper hut or in a completed part of the building? On bigger sites, is there a checker keeping tally?
4 What is the condition of the access roads? Are they reasonably free from mud and kept clear of rubbish?
5 Are the site huts and offices sensibly arranged, organized and kept clean?

Examine the building work and gain an impression of the following:

6 Standard of concrete.
7 Standard of brickwork and blockwork.
8 Standard of carpentry and joinery.
9 The degree of protection of finished work from the transit of materials to and fro.
10 Is completed accommodation locked up securely?

What is your impression of the morale and application of the men working on site?

11 Are those present working? Are people leaving early?
12 Are tea breaks under control?
13 Are there jobs which could be done which would last for a reasonable period to which men could be applied? In other words, are work-interfaces left unoccupied?

14 Is scaffolding being properly employed, or left idle?

Any experienced architect, engineer or builder will under-stand the nature of such a visit. A good impression can be obtained without the necessity of going through a check list. Sampling is a respectable way of gauging the state of practical operations and for building sites it is very revealing. If you are the building owner and your impression of these things is less than good, then probably you are not getting value for money and you may be in danger of getting poorer quality, loss of time and extra costs. By correct organization, these things can be rectified.

2

Principles

Before launching into a description of the functions, dos and don'ts, of each of those involved in building management on site, it will save time if the principles common to all are set out once, so that they do not have to be repeated in each chapter. They are important, but they are often ignored, and then inefficiency results. An understanding of them is essential.

Objectives

The whole process should be informed by the desire to build the best possible building for the client in a manner which suits him, at a cost he can afford and as quickly as possible to save valuable time.

The objectives can be set out as follows:

- *Cost*
  The building must be good value for money. Estimates and tenders must be reliable. Authorized extras must be kept under strict control.

- *Quality*
  This should be consistent with the standards paid for. Contrary to popular view, there is no lack of skill but most of

the problems occur from lack of care, and this is consequent upon the lack of proper supervision and concern (as has been described in the Bentley Report).

- *Time*
  The programme should be the best minimum obtainable. The value of time saved is part of the basic economics of the development.

- *Design*
  The building must suit the client's needs in every particular within the constraints of the budget. It must be appropriate to the site. Within these limits it is desirable that it should have an architectural quality which adds to the quality of its environment and can be enjoyed as much as possible by its occupants.

Communication breaks

The orthodox processes of managing a building job, from the time the client has the original proposal in his mind to the craftsmen fabricating the building on site, involve on average, twelve steps. At each of these steps there is an attenuation of communication of some sort. This may be either a transference of a written brief into a drawing, or the interpretation of drawings and notes into technical measurements and special descriptions in the bills of quantity. Sometimes these breaks occur because a new group of people take over the process, as for instance when the site agent receives the first batch of drawings and the bills of quantities. Figure 2.1 illustrates the communications chain. This may differ in individual cases. In practice the number of breaks is many more than twelve. The work is referred back up the line to the client for approval. It can be referred back to local authorities over planning problems, and on a variety of other occasions. The number of actual breaks that occur may average twenty-five.

Such breaks in communication are clearly a disadvantage and reduce the efficiency of the building process to a marked degree. When things go wrong, 'authority' is always inclined to insert another tier of supervisors, project managers or other officials,

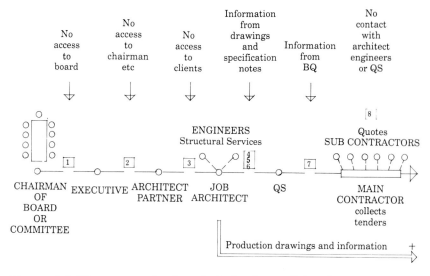

Figure 2.1 *The communication chain in the traditional system.*

when probably the real error is that the teams could cope if only they had been selected properly in the first place. It is possible to reduce the breaks to three, and Figure 2.2 indicates one such example. Another variation of a shortened communication chain occurs in the various types of package deal which are discussed more fully in chapter 3 on the role of the client. It does not follow that the shortened forms are necessarily better. They are only as good as the people running them and their motivation in relation to the client's best interests.

It will be seen that in the orthodox process of managing building there is a tendency for middlemen of various sorts to come between the exponents. They emerge in the first place because they can offer some rationalization of the cost or of the organization, but in the end there is a tendency for them merely to take a percentage without particular benefit and sometimes they even obfuscate straightforward solutions.

Drawings

We produce too many drawings. We can trace the reason for this in the lack of direct relationships and trust between designers,

TRADITIONAL – BREAKS IN COMMUNICATION (cont'd.)

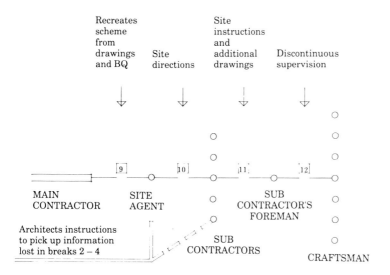

engineers, craftsmen and technicians. As will be seen, modern forms of contract academically and arbitrarily separate out the construction process from design. The best and most creative craftsmanship arises when the designer and the craftsman work closely together. As a potent example of this, an eighteenth century church or great house required on average about twelve drawings, and the work rested on a firm relationship between the architect and the master craftsmen. Today those same buildings would take hundreds, if not thousands of drawings and it is unlikely that the creative quality of the craftsmanship could ever match that produced by our Georgian forebears. (See the portfolios at the RIBA Drawings Collection).

Drawings must be prepared with the recipient primarily in mind. He may be the client, seeking to understand how the building will measure up to his operations; the planning authority who seek to see how the building conforms to the planning policy; or the craftsman who needs to understand how the building goes together, in the clearest possible way. At times drawings are prepared as an academic work of art, full of technical references and codes which are beyond the ordinary tradesman on site.

Specifications

Not so long ago, architects would write specifications describing in detail the materials and work which would be required in every part of the job. At the least they produced specification notes which others could engross into a satisfactory document. Nowadays this vital and useful task has diminished, to the disadvantage of the contractors but also from the point of view of clarifying the work in the designer's mind. Computers are now coming into architects' and engineers' offices to such an extent and with such power that much of the drudgery can now be removed from the work of specification writing.

As with drawings, it is easy to write technically abstruse specifications referring to various British Standards, Agrément Certificates, Codes of Practice, etc. To the storeman in the ironmonger's shop or the craftsman on site, such references may not mean a great deal. Care should be taken to see that the message is appropriate to the recipient. There are other methods of quantifying the work and describing the standards, together with discussion and negotiation with reputable suppliers and trade contractors, that can short cut a lot of documentation.

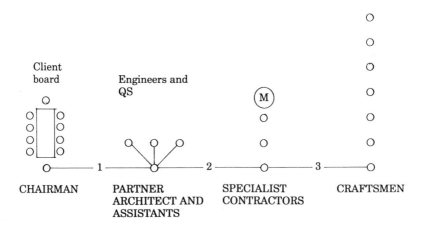

Figure 2.2 *The shortened communication chain in Advanced Methods of Management (AMM).* Ⓜ *= Manager.*

Bills of Quantities

The quantity surveyor translates the information contained in the drawings and specification into Bills of Quantities (BQ) using the Standard Method of Measurement. These descriptions of labour and materials, together with their measurements, are primarily designed to be a standard basis upon which tenders from different contractors are obtained. It is not a document designed for the purpose of ordering materials or programming labour, nor is it necessarily written in the language appropriate to some of the trades and, indeed, it has to be retranslated by them for the purposes of their estimating. Thus it can be seen that, although it is a relatively expensive document to produce (3½% of the contract sum), it has limited application. There is also a tendency in the industry to stretch its use for these other purposes. In terms of ease of communication there is another difficulty in that the standard language used is fine for experienced estimators and quantity surveyors, but is understood only partially by architects, and hardly at all by clients and some tradesmen.

As computer power increases in architects', surveyors' and engineers' offices, so these problems can be overcome. But they will only be successful if the authors of the programs concerned make sure that the language of the print-outs can be clearly understood by clients and craftsmen. Other ways of scheduling the work will be described in detail later.

Instructions

As work on site proceeds these can take at least five forms, that is: drawings, variation orders, architects instructions, letters and minutes of meetings. To get a complete picture of a problem, it is often necessary to research all five means of communication and confusion can arise.

Authorized communications line

Apart from run-of-the-mill orthodox work, where most of the content can be foreseen and allowed for at the outset, there are many jobs where the work has to be done in an evolving situation, for example: in factories where work has to continue on the production line whilst alterations are being carried out, or where a building is being provided for a new process which has not been completely developed. In these dynamic cases, a sole link has to be formed between a director of the client organization who is held responsible by his board for the project, and the chairman of the executive side of the building organization. This line may go through the architects or engineers. It is important that this is established at the outset. The short circuiting or the breaking of such a line can be damaging to the process.

Personal relations (Human dynamics)

People work effectively and efficiently together for a variety of reasons which can be identified and catered for. It is no use throwing people together because they have the right qualifications and happen to be available. As Robert Heller says in *The Business of Winning* people and organizations alike will probably not approach their potential unless:

- They know what they are supposed to be doing.
- They are capable of doing it.
- They are given the environment and the resources needed to do the job.
- They are encouraged to succeed.
- They are rewarded for their success.

Self-motivation versus pressure

For a team activity, and the construction of a building is a good example, one can either be optimistic about human nature and design the positive environment to encourage self-motivation, choosing particular team members who are most likely to thrive in such an atmosphere, or alternatively one can be more cynical and decide to drive people by various forms of pressure.

Heller summarizes the positive attributes as follows:

- The expenditure of physical and mental effort in work is as natural as play or rest.
- People will exercise self-direction and self-control in the service of objectives to which they are committed.
- People's commitment to objectives is a function of the rewards associated with their achievement.
- The average person learns, under proper conditions, not only to accept but to seek responsibility.

The negative approach can be summarized as follows:

- The average person has an inherent dislike of work and will avoid it if possible.
- Because of their dislike of work, most people must be coerced, controlled, directed or threatened with punishment to get them to make adequate effort.
- The average person prefers to be directed, wishes to avoid responsibility, has relatively little ambition and wants security above all else.

In real life, effective organizations may work entirely on the positive line but sometimes there is a mixture, e.g. where there is a negative line taken by the managing director but where the departmental directors have sufficient latitude to control their own areas without undue interference. In terms of the building process, experience indicates that the positive line is the most effective so long as everyone appreciates that failure to achieve reasonable targets of cost, time or quality, will result in duplication or replacement. The client, after all, is paying good money and has a right to expect good control.

Size of teams

The key to a successful job lies with the design and management team. Not only should the members of the team be sufficiently qualified and experienced, and have positive motivation, but they must also be temperamentally compatible. To have one key individual in a team with whom the others find it difficult to work reduces the efficiency of that team to an unacceptable degree. Temperamental compatibility is not easily measurable. Personal interviews go somewhere towards it, but a 'shake down' period is necessary, during which a careful eye must be kept upon this important aspect of relationships. The risk of incompatibilities rises markedly with the number of relationships in the team. Figure 2.3 indicates how the number of relationships increases dramatically with relatively small increases in the numbers of people. Where the number of relationships increases to significantly more than about 30 (6 people), the chances of an incompatibility become significant. This is why large teams invariably have problems of temperament within them.

Figure 2.3 indicates the unitary relationships – in other words the relationships between individuals only. There is a much larger number of relationships if groups of 2, 3, 4 etc. are considered both with all the other individuals and with all the other permutations of groups. This is relevant for it is often the case in committees that one group will be at odds with another group within the committee.

A practical way of reducing the risk is as follows:

1 Do not choose teams by dictat, rather allow the nucleus members of the team to become part of the interviewing and selecting process for the remaining members.
2 For the first month of the operation make a special point of sounding out team members views on how co-operation and positive attitudes are developing within the group. If an incompatibility emerges, remove the odd-ball immediately. Transfer him to another site, another job or another office, but act swiftly. Do not operate this technique without

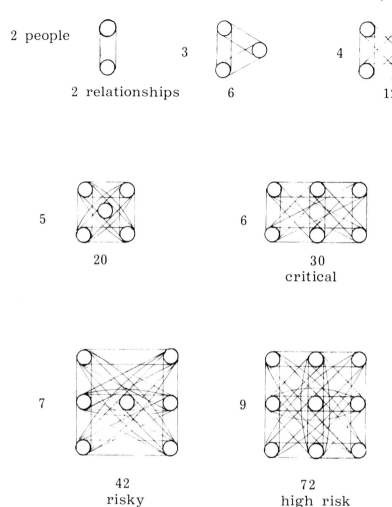

Figure 2.3 *Chances of incompatibility rise with the size of the team, as the number of individual relationships increases at an increasing rate with each additional member.*

compassion, remember he may fit in perfectly well in a different team.

Qualifications

It is conventional wisdom to call for a certain level of qualification when selecting candidates for a particular operation.

Qualifications are a short-cut aid to selection and in using them as a criterion one should remember that one is depending upon the assessment of academic examiners, and the peculiar skill of passing exams itself may not be sufficient. Everyone knows of cases of unqualified people who are better performers than their qualified brethren. However, qualifications should not be disregarded as they are a valuable guide.

Experience

In the building process experience is invaluable but it must be of the right sort in terms of both organization and building type. One should look for an attitude and a willingness in the candidate to extend his or her range. In taking any such step, however, the proposed new field should not be beyond reach. It is common in the building industry for the good craftsman to be promoted to site agent. The two jobs are very different. Many site agents have been demoralized by being unable to cope with the promotion. A period of training and/or understudying would have saved the failure and consequent demoralization.

Age

It is encouraging occasionally to discover cases where comparatively young and inexperienced people have been able to measure up to more senior colleagues and to be accepted as valuable team contributors. Such success depends very much upon the temperament of the individual and his ability to say when he does not know the answer, and for his colleagues to be prepared to make allowances and give him a hand. The enthusiasm and flexibility of mind of younger members of the team can be an invaluable contribution to the success of the job.

Chain strength

The strength of a chain is that of its weakest link and this is particularly true of teams or groups working in the building industry at whatever level. It is particularly important in the case of the site management team. If one weak member is permitted to stay in the team he is inevitably the one who will be the focus of problems. It is of no help to the team or to the service of the client to allow him to stay there, nor indeed, is it in his own personal interest.

Hierarchical structures reduce operating efficiency

An example of the structure of a large architects department in a well known authority is shown in Figure 2.4, which only represents the architectural side and does not indicate the parallel departments of quantity surveying, structural engineering and services engineering. It does indicate the parallel administrative department which sits 'alongside' the professional people. In some cases the professional people were isolated from the elected committees of members at the points of decision by the administrative people. They were also isolated from a senior direction by intermediate levels in the hierarchy and these two elements caused great frustration and loss of

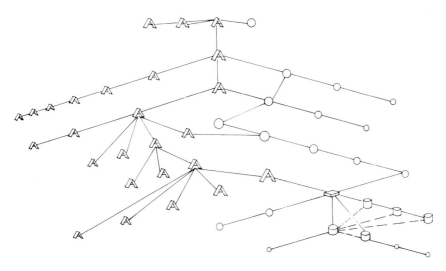

Figure 2.4 *Hierarchical structures in a large department can reduce operating efficiency.*

effectiveness. Furthermore, hours allocated to any architectural task had to be diminished by the cost of the 'hierarchs', the non-operational levels in the tiers above them.

Leading role

The leader of the building team on site may be an architect or engineer, depending upon the way the contract has been set up. It is important to understand the real nature of professional leadership, which is quite different from the term 'leadership' as understood in other fields, such as in the army or in seafaring. Assuming that each member of the team has the same objectives, then the actual role of leadership changes as the input changes. If the item under review is that of cost, then the quantity surveyor or estimator will hold the floor and illuminate the priorities. So long as all the members realize that he is being fair, not only to his own firm, but to the client's interest, his contribution to the problem will be respected. When the subject changes, say to that of the use of the building in relation to a particular space, then

Figure 2.5 *Conflicting viewpoints for the client.*

Figure 2.6 *Teamwork solutions.*

the architect's contribution will be the leading input at that particular stage. So the leadership role changes from member to member. There has, however, to be a chairman who ensures that the whole team continues to progress along the right general track.

The team cannot work successfully if members of the team have differing objectives. If the site agent has been instructed by his directors to make the most of his claims file then he will be inclined to hold out for extras, extensions to the programme, etc. which other members of the team will find irritating and negative. The chairman of the team will automatically be the person selected by the organizational method determined by the client through his choice of structure (Chapter 3). If the contract is an orthodox one, then this will probably be a contracts manager or a site agent. If however, it is a professionally managed job, then it will be an architect or an engineer, alternatively it may be directed by an architect with a full time site team of project architect and construction manager.

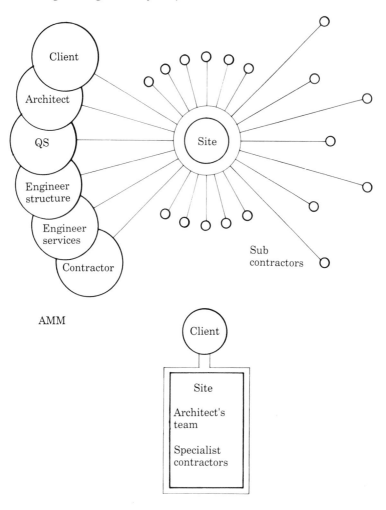

Figure 2.7 *Alternative approaches to the geographical location of offices.*

Site meetings

Successful jobs will have a pace which the participants will find stimulating and, to a degree, enjoyable. Conversely a job which drags out its programme can be boring and enervating. Though some jobs can theoretically be run without site meetings, much in reality does depend upon successful relationships between the designers, site agents and trade contractors. This engenders co-operation and sensible decision making. One of the best vehicles for producing these attitudes is to have regular site meetings, for which there are certain important rules:

1 No meeting should last more than one and a quarter hours.
2 It should not be a post mortem of errors.
3 It should review the present situation of the works so that everybody understands the practical position.
4 The immediate programme of activity should be gone over, with everybody given a sensible chance to contribute and to raise any problems which they foresee.
5 Every consultant and every trade that is directly involved should be represented by the most senior person possible. It is an advantage to have the client attending, (though there are certain provisos).
6 The minutes should be taken by the chairman or the project architect and should be dictated, typed and issued immediately after the meeting. It is also possible to make a manuscript note of the meeting and to photocopy it immediately afterwards. Immediacy is the essence, so that participants can have an early note of what needs to be done.
7 Minutes should always be agreed as the first item of the succeeding meeting and the record signed. They should be distributed to every firm or individual concerned with the job even though they may not immediately be involved at that particular stage.
8 On direct professional control jobs it is preferable to make the minutes the comprehensive record of the job so that there is one complete story officially acknowledged from start to finish. Others prefer to make architects instructions or the site-book rank for the official record. However, as everyone receives copies of the minutes and they are officially agreed each week or each month, they are the best continuing record.
9 A copy of the minutes can, if necessary, be cannibalized each week or each month, so that a continuous record can be put together for each section of the works.

Geographic spread

On a conventional site there is a degree of inefficiency attributable to the geographic spread of the offices of all those concerned. The problem of bringing them all together to make an effective site organization involves much travelling and may give rise to opportunities for miscommunication. On a recent job, by no means unusual, the client's offices were in London W1, the contractors in Sidcup, Kent, the architects in Bristol, the structural engineer in Plymouth, the trade contractors from Liverpool, Bristol, Birmingham and London, and the site was in Swindon. On such a job, if a problem occurs of any significance and a meeting has to be called, there are consequent delays not only in calling the meeting but in co-ordinating the drawings and valuations before any revision or alteration can take place on the site. The delays to the trade contractors, through hold-ups in information, account for a significant decrease in efficiency. During such delays, trade contractors may find it too costly to hold on site the operatives concerned and they have to be deployed elsewhere. When the approved variation order is issued to site, the new operatives have to pick up where the others left off. This in itself, causes inefficiency during the period the new men start the learning curve. (Figure 2.8).

It follows that any reduction in the effects of geographical spread is helpful. One approach is to look for good local firms whenever possible. Another more concentrated solution is to form site teams, as in an AMM type organization that looks towards bringing together a full time professional team with the important members of the significant trade contracting teams, who are also full time on site.

Full time commitment

A competent architect or engineer in a good practice at any one time will be looking after a number of jobs, most of which are at different stages. A sampling of the incoming telephone calls to a typical professional office will give an indication as to the wide

TRADITIONAL   AMM

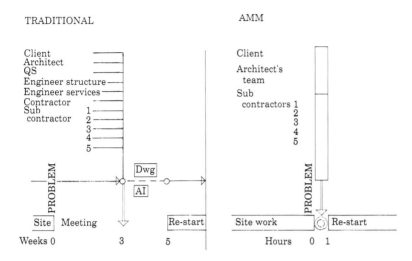

Figure 2.8 *In traditional arrangements a problem on site involving several trades may impose weeks of delay while meetings are arranged and revised details are issued, meanwhile key workers may be moved off site, whereas a permanent on-site team can resolve the problem without significant breaks in the work.*

cast of problems that he has to have in mind at any one time. Contracts managers often spend more time in the car travelling from site to site than on working on schemes. Site agents, similarly, often have two or three jobs to look after during their average working week. This continual 'grasshoppering' reduces average efficiency and, what may be even more important, reduces the capacity of the individual to give time to the prediction of problems and solutions. Hence, wherever possible, it is advisable to concentrate people full time on sites. As a very rough guide a job of £1m can afford a full time site architect and certainly a full time agent. A job of £2k can afford daily visits by the architect. A job of £1m with normal structural frame can afford a full time site engineer for the appropriate period. Schemes with a large input, of, say, mechanical services can require the services trade contractor to supply an on-site management team. There are methods of employing high-grade people for this type of work which will be discussed in the appropriate chapters. The great benefit of a full time on-site presence of the site management team is that there is a quick reaction to problems coming along the line. It is always better to predict problems than to wait until the difficulties arise.

Value of preparatory work

Pre-contract work should be evaluated and graded by experienced people, in order to determine:

1 Design and preparatory work which must be done before work on site commences so as to make the most efficient use of resources.
2 Design and preparatory work which can *safely* be left to a later stage so that advantage can be taken of the build-up of knowledge about function and form.

It is now conventional to assume that all design and preparatory work must be treated as (1) above, when in point of fact a proportion of most jobs can be treated as (2). A proper analysis will make for a building of more satisfactory performance and will enable the client to tune the building more closely to his operation. At the beginning of work on site, except in the case of repeat jobs, no one has a complete understanding of the building. Understanding matures as the contract proceeds, and it is therefore important to allocate suitable work into category (2).

However, as much design work as possible should be carried out before work starts, graded to the nature of the design operation, i.e. there are those design operations which are related to the whole building and a hierarchy of others which relate to sections of the building, right down to the smallest detail. Each not only has its functional priority but has also a time scale within the design process. Within the ordering of the design work it is important that each stage is as complete as possible, for every pound spent on the design stage controls ten pounds spent on site. It follows that, if insufficient effort is made at the design stage, then work on site will be consequently ill-considered and wasteful and, as likely as not, to the wrong standard.

There may be problems relating to the form of contract which may inhibit a sensible spread of work. It may be in the interest of the contractor to demand information prematurely, with the consequence that the architect/engineer cannot comply with a heavy schedule of drawings and documents at short notice. Non-compliance then forms the basis of a claim for extra payment under the contract. It is therefore wise for the architect/ engineer to prepare a programme setting out the drawings and documents with their proposed dates of issue, which is included in the tender documents. The contractor is required to adjust his prices accordingly. (Provision for this is made in the ACA form of contract, 2nd Edition).

Value of time

Much of the work on site can be run in parallel. There is a convention, which is somewhat misplaced, that much of the building work has to be organized serially, i.e. one operation must finish before the next starts, which accounts for the inordinate length of time that some building contracts now take. It is sometimes possible, by carefully studying the potentiality for time saving by parallel working, to reduce contract times by as much as 50%. The criteria for such organization is set out later. However, the examples overleaf of the value of time are pertinent. It is worth using these examples to test the value of time for each development proposition that comes forward. More impressive savings are made in the case of rehabilitation jobs on valuable city sites.

Significant time can be saved in the period during which permissions are received from the authorities, which will be dealt with in detail later. For instance, there may be no need to wait until formal building act or building regulation approvals are received except in certain cases: e.g. 'Ex-Section 20' buildings in London. Every good professional firm should discuss problems and interpretations with building control officers and know how to conform to the law. The only difficulties which may emerge at the end are differences in detailed interpretation. If the client is made aware that there is a small percentage risk, say, that the fire officer may change his mind over the need for an extra fire door, then the time saved in

The value of time saving.

Example 2.1

18 Month Contract

Cost of site	2,000,000	
Interest over 18 mths @ say 13% a.p.r.	390,000	
Cost of construction 1,000 m² @ £900/m² (contract sum)	900,000	
Allowance for inflation on tenders	45,000	
Interest on construction		
£945,000 × $\dfrac{13\%}{2}$ × 1½ yrs	92,150	
	3,427,150	3,427,150

9 Month Contract

Cost of site	2,000,000	
Interest over 9 mths @ say 13% a.p.r.	195,000	
Cost of construction	900,000	
Allowance for inflation on tenders	22,500	
Interest on construction		
£922,500 × $\dfrac{13\%}{2}$ × ¾ yr	45,000	
	3,162,500	
Less –		
Rent or value earnt by earlier occupation		
£350 × 800 m² × $\dfrac{9}{12}$	210,000	
	2,952,500	2,952,500
Saving:		£474,650

or 51% of the
contract sum

proceeding before receipt of approval is usually well worth it. Similarly many of the building trade operations can be run in parallel. The techniques involved will be described at the appropriate place. However, by far the most significant amount of time lost during the process is that taken up with the legal side of the purchase of the site. Time, in this area, is usually measured

The value of time saving.

Example 2.2

18 Month Contract

Cost of existing building	5,000,000	
Interest over 18 mths @ say 13% a.p.r.	975,000	
Cost of rehabilitation	2,000,000	
Allowance for inflation on tenders	100,000	
Interest on rehabilitation		
$£2,100,000 \times \dfrac{13\%}{2} \times 1\tfrac{1}{2}$ yrs	204,750	
	8,279,750	8,279,750

6 Month Contract

Cost of existing building	5,000,000	
Interest over 6 mths @ say 13% a.p.r.	325,000	
Cost of rehabilitation	2,000,000	
Allowance for inflation on tenders	30,000	
Interest on rehabilitation		
$£2,030,000 \times \dfrac{13\%}{2} \times \tfrac{1}{2}$ yr	66,000	
	7,421,000	
Less –		
Rent or value earnt by earlier occupation		
$£350 \times 2,000$ m^2 $\times$ 1 yr	700,000	
	6,721,000	6,721,000
Saving:		£ 1,558,750
		or 77% of the contract sum

in years rather than weeks. The total loss to building owners and to the community is immense. This is an area where other real improvements can be made but is beyond the scope of this book.

Full use of work interfaces

Site management can make a major contribution by ensuring that effort is fully engaged in all those areas where work can be continued for a reasonable period. Two-dimensional charts or programmes are insufficient to illuminate these areas and it takes a three-dimensional imagination to perceive the potentialities.

It is important for the whole team to appreciate that as the quality of information improves the closer its production can be programmed to its need on site. This is related to the increase in the number of active participants, the three-dimensional appreciation of the application situation, and the realization of urgency. The quality of information has several modes. The maximum effort should be released at the appropriate time, in the appropriate detail and on the right target. For instance there is little point in releasing the ironmongery schedule at the same time as the bar bending schedules, for as the client learns more about the uses of his building so his input concerning the adjustment of ironmongery schedules will improve with time. Much rescheduling can be avoided if the information is released at the *appropriate* time. Building information can be imagined as a tree-like structure growing upwards from the 'strategic' trunk to the 'intermediate' boughs and towards the 'detailed' leaves.

A teamwork programme can and should be prepared at an early stage, of which the following is an example.

Stage I Strategic
    Scheme design.
    Frame and foundations.
    Site work.
    Material and workmanship standards.
    Cost plan.
    Mechanical services outline.

Stage II Intermediate
    As the work on Stage I proceeds on site, the early stages of the work are taken to greater detail and specifications prepared, and further work is done on equipment and finishes.

Stage III Detail

As Stage II proceeds on site, the detail of the landscape scheme is prepared, partition layouts discussed and settled with the building owner, special furniture is agreed upon, designed and detailed.

Each stage of the work must be given time for high-level input and detailed coverage. This, as seen above, can stretch well into the operational process on site. Rushing the design, strategic or intermediate or detailed, is bound to cause a waste of money and resources in its geared effect upon the work on site.

Similarly it must be emphasized that the rushing of tendering through the main contractor procedure or, in AMM, the trade contractor procedure, (as described later) will inevitably involve inadequate consideration by the estimators in all those companies concerned. This will mean that the figures will include unnecessary cover prices which will inflate the cost of the building. So adequate time must always be given to tendering. It is very much a false economy to cut down this stage.

Layered information

With CAD and overlay drafting (Figure 2.9 and page 90 *et seq*) it is not difficult for the professional team to prepare drawings containing information only relevant to a particular recipient, e.g. building regulations officials, fire prevention officers, landscape specialists etc. There is a danger lurking in a slavish following of this layering approach, in that the co-ordination of trades can fail, e.g. door swings and radiators with socket outlets behind, or duct terminals positioned awkwardly in tiling or panelling.

It is vital for site architects/engineers to check frequently at operative level that the most up-to-date drawing revision is being used. Out of date drawings must be eliminated. On large jobs information stations around the scheme should be updated daily by a responsible individual.

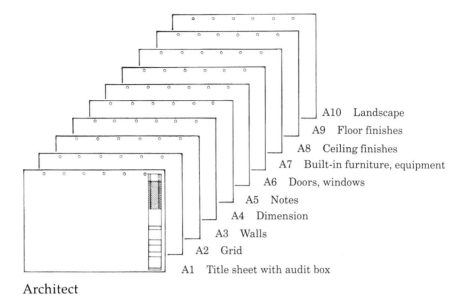

A10   Landscape
A9   Floor finishes
A8   Ceiling finishes
A7   Built-in furniture, equipment
A6   Doors, windows
A5   Notes
A4   Dimension
A3   Walls
A2   Grid
A1   Title sheet with audit box

Architect

E4   Stairs/special features
E3   Columns – and beams
E2   Foundations
E1   Architects composite of: A1, A2, A3, A4, A8, A9

Structural Engineer

Figure 2.9 *The use of overlay drafting.*

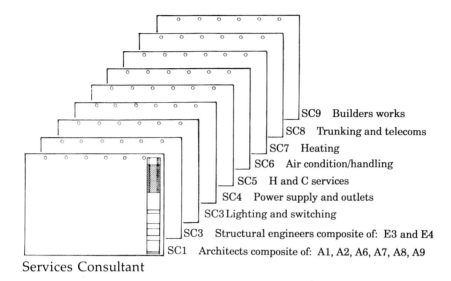

SC9   Builders works
SC8   Trunking and telecoms
SC7   Heating
SC6   Air condition/handling
SC5   H and C services
SC4   Power supply and outlets
SC3 Lighting and switching
SC3   Structural engineers composite of: E3 and E4
SC1   Architects composite of: A1, A2, A6, A7, A8, A9

Services Consultant

Tendering procedure and packages

Most of the work is now tendered for, the only exceptions being those skills or supplies which are unique. On fast track the package process is usual. Each tenderable entity, e.g. windows, doors, precast units, is drawn, specified and measured. The package is completed with the trade contract form and sent to the agreed short-listed firms. Each firm is visited before receiving the package by the tender supervision team consisting of architect/engineer, estimator/QS, construction manager and sometimes the client's representative, to gauge the attitude of directors and staff, and the condition of plant. A financial viability check is made (Dunn & Bradstreet). At mid-tender stage the firms are individually called in to clear up misunderstandings, take on board improvements etc. There is a post tender interview to finalize price and time, and sign up. Regrettably six weeks is needed for this process, which is a painfully long slice out of the real programme of work, but it cannot be curtailed for good package tendering is the key to economy and quality.

One problem with packages from the professional team's point of view is that advanced sections are wanted earlier and can be demanded before the general arrangement drawings have been properly co-ordinated in plan, section and elevation combining structural, services and other specialist input. Rushed or premature packages are bound to lead to bodges.

Contract

The object of a 'form of agreement' (contract) is to arrange between the principal parties, the client (building owner) and the builders (contractors) firstly, what is to be built for how much money, and in what time; and secondly, to set out what are the rights and remedies of the parties in the face of problems and difficulties.

Ideally the contract, once signed, should be put in a drawer and not looked at again. If there are positive attitudes on both sides from the outset, then this can happen. Building is a prime example of co-operative enterprise, and should not therefore be prone to legalistic wrangles aimed at screwing every extra penny out of the client, or unreasonably demanding extra work not tendered for from the contractors.

The contract should set out the following:

- *'Articles of Agreement'* (From a draft by Geoffrey Trickey FRICS ACIArb, Partner, Davis Langdon & Everest, quantity surveyors, but with the author's modifications)

1 Date of Contract.
2 Names of Parties.
3 Brief description of work.
4 Brief description of contract documents.
5 Name of architect/engineer.
6 Name of quantity surveyor or cost consultant (if appointed).
7 Agreement on carrying out the works and the sum to be paid.
8 Restrictions on assignment by either party.

- *Contract Conditions*

1 Contractor's obligations: use of diligence; scope and standard of work; compliance with statutory requirements; completion date; remedy for failure (i.e. employ others); defects liability, insurance.

2 Architect's duties: to include – issue of further data in accordance with the programme; issue of variations; dealing with discrepancies; removal of defective work or men and making good defects other than by removal; restriction on hours, site boundaries; testing; etc.

3 Extensions of time and damages including act or default of the employer and matters beyond the control or assessment of either party which can be grounds for extension of the time or can be valued by the architect/engineer or quantity surveyor in fair valuation.

4 Valuations of variations/remeasurement: these can be measured in advance in accordance with agreed rates or their projected equivalent.

5 Payment: Interim and Final and the provision for retention; fluctuations and their valuation.

6 Termination: by employer/contractor.

7 Provisions for VAT and tax deduction.

8 Arbitration.

The contract should *not* contain (as many do) the following:

1 Matters which are better covered by common law;

2 Matters which can be more simply dealt with by exchange of letters;

3 Management procedures;

4 Words or phrases which an inexperienced client or a foreman/chargehand would find difficult to understand.

In his tender, the contractor should allow for any specialist sub-contractor specified in the contract documents. He should have the right of approval of any specialist sub-contractor required by the architect/engineer after the contract has been signed.

Similarly, the architect should have the right of approval in sufficient time of domestic (i.e. the contractor's own) sub-contractors, and should have the right of free access to them, for it is possible for the main contractor to prevent such access in order to increase potentiality of claims for extra payments. Trade contractors often are able to contribute improvements in the construction, efficiency or economy of a job, which should go to the benefit of the client.

Where a main contractor is not employed, the agreement with trade contractors can be covered by letter. An example is given at the end of this chapter.

The form of contract most commonly used is that produced by the JCT (Joint Contracts Tribunal), mistakenly often referred to as the 'RIBA Contract'. The tribunal, which is a drafting committee (wrongly called a tribunal), consists of representatives of twelve of the bodies which make up the building industry, e.g. architects, surveyors, builders, suppliers, trade contractors, etc. Clients have not been directly represented until recently. Over the years, as JCT edition succeeds JCT edition, so more and more of the risks inherent in the process of building have been removed from the contractor and have been placed on the client's shoulders – he who is least experienced and least able to assess them. There is now a trend toward a better balance. As the contract should be *fair* agreement, efforts must be made to rectify as far as possible the defects mentioned above.

The JCT may produce a radical improvement on the unsatisfactory JCT '80 *et seq*. The Association of Consultant Architects (ACA) Contract goes some way to solving the problems. The JCT Small Works Contract is useful but does not allow for fluctuations in prices. In spite of its title, it can be used for larger contracts, say up to £5m so long as the term is short. However, it does contain redundant material.

The JCT have recently produced their Intermediate Form of Contract, which in many ways is a better document. It does not contain the elaborate provisions for nomination nor provisions for fluctuations, so, whilst this is a satisfactory document in certain circumstances, it does have its problems.

Another form of contract is GC/Works/l, which is used mainly by government departments. It gives wide powers to the 'supervising officer' who has the final say in much of the work. This can cause contractors to 'cover' the risk of eccentric judgement and can make tenders unnecessarily high. It has no claims history!

The contract used by the structural engineers is intended mainly for construction engineering and is not really sufficient for general building work.

Example letter of agreement

A typical letter of agreement for professionally managed small works, separate trades contracts, (known as the 'SAMM contract'), by Patrick Emett FRICS.

It should be modified by the architect/engineer to suit the circumstances of each particular job.

Dear Sirs

I refer to your quotation dated ....

On behalf of our client, ...

I am pleased to inform you of their formal acceptance of your quotation.
Your accounts should be addressed to ....
but sent to this office for our certification in the normal manner and subsequent direct payment by our client.

The work is to be carried out as directed by this firm to our satisfaction and subject to the following conditions.

Any variation to your quotation will be confirmed in writing, either by letter, architect's instruction or as recorded in the site meeting minutes. The final account of your work will therefore be adjusted if necessary for any addition or omission from this original order.

Kindly note that you are to comply with all necessary notices required statute, any statutory instrument, rule or order or any regulation or by-law applicable to your work and in particular your works should comply with all current safety at work and health regulations and enactments and any legislation which should come into operation during the currency of your work under the contract.

At all these times you should keep on site a competent person in charge of your operations.

The work must not be sub-let without our written permission.

Please advise us of your programme for the work and anticipated completion date.

If it becomes apparent that you will not be able to complete the work within the contract programme, without prior approval or reasonable cause, then we reserve the right to cancel the order or supplement your labour and/or material from another source and to set off the costs of this section pro-rata to the work carried out.

You will be liable for and shall indemnify the employer against any liability, loss, claim or proceedings whatsoever arising out of any statute or a common law in respect of personal injury or death. You shall maintain such insurances as are necessary to cover this liability. You shall also similarly indemnify the employer against any damage to real or to personal property including the works to an amount of £1m in so far as the damage arises out of the works being carried out by you due to negligence, omission or default.

Please ensure that you have all the necessary insurances as given above.

You shall be responsible for materials delivered to the site but unfixed except where they are delivered into the employers store and we would expect you to make good any deficiencies that may arise from whatever cause.

The works will be insured by the building owner in respect of fire, lightning, explosion, storm, tempest, flood, bursting or overflowing water tanks, apparatus or pipes, earthquake, aircraft or other aerial device or articles dropped therefrom, riot and civil commotion. If any loss should occur from any of the above causes an inventory of cost should be sent to us as soon as practicable.

We will issue a certificate showing the date when we consider the works to be practicably complete. Any defect that arises within the period of 6 months from the date of practical completion shall be rectified by you and entirely at your own expense.

Interim payments may be made at any time reasonably requested by you and a payment shall be made for the total value of the work completed and all materials delivered within a reasonable time and not prematurely, less a retention of 5% which shall be released half at practical completion and the balance after the defects liability period and making good any defects. Payment will be made within fourteen days of certification.

All persons employed on the works shall be paid in accordance with the fair wages resolution or any amendment or statute relating thereto.

This contract for provision of services to the works shall be determined due to bankruptcy or if any arrangement is made with creditors before a winding up order has been passed in connection with the business or for any reason of negligence through failure to proceed diligently with the works or to make good defective work.

In all matters relating to the work, you shall abide by the Prevention of Corruption Act 1889 and 1916.

Should any dispute or difference arise which cannot reasonably be settled by this firm or any matter upon which you have a grievance, an arbitrator shall be appointed by the President of the Institute of Arbitrators.

You are to supply any necessary messing arrangements for your own work people.

You are to supply any necessary tool boxes or other locked storage for tools and materials as you may deem necessary, except as otherwise advised. You will be responsible for unloading your own materials etc. You should satisfy yourselves as to the security of the premises and advise us of any additional requirements.

Ensure that your work people do not damage other existing or new work and should damage occur it is to be rectified at your own expense to our satisfaction.

Value Added Tax should be added to the tender sum at the standard rate unless the work has been deemed to be zero rated.

Please supply a copy of certificate showing you have the necessary documentation under the construction industry as deduction scheme issued by H M Inspector of Taxes.

The quotation is a fixed price and not subject to adjustment for increasing costs, unless otherwise agreed.

Unless otherwise agreed the materials used shall be in accordance with the relevant British Standard and workmanship shall be of good quality to produce a finished product of sufficiently high standard to be acceptable to the architect and building owner. We will be pleased to answer any query regarding the standard of finish required.

Yours faithfully

3
The client

The client, otherwise known, particularly in contract documents, as 'the building owner' or 'the employer' has the most critical role to play in the production of the building: that of electing the method, negotiating the finance, choosing the architect and his team, deciding the brief and encouraging the enterprise of construction. Above and beyond all this, he is the patron of architecture, and thus is able to contribute in a practical way to the way our civilization expresses itself in the built form. His decisions will affect the quality of life of those who work in, live in or visit his building, and the building itself will contribute to the character of the locality in which it is placed. Thus he is more important than the architect or the contractors and his name should appear on the site board so that all can see who has shouldered the responsibility. It is then possible for his name to be celebrated where the building is a success for those who live and work in it and for those who experience it as part of the environment. It is better for an individual's name to be identified in this way, rather than that of some impersonal organization. Such is the practice in some Scandinavian countries and has an undoubted beneficial effect upon the quality of architecture and its enjoyment.

The nature of choice

Decisions concerning the need for a building are usually made by a committee, or less often, an individual. Often there is some doubt as to whether an existing building should be rehabilitated or whether new work is required. It is then useful to commission a firm of architects to prepare a report showing the possibilities and costs of the alternatives. It may be that the firm or department selected for this work will succeed naturally to the design and organization of the building work to follow. In any case it is essential to take considerable care and trouble in the selection of the firm. For from this choice flows the success, mediocrity or failure of the result. There are a large number of good architects available as well as those of other sorts. Clients can seek the advice of the Clients' Advisory Service at the RIBA or they can refer to the *ACA Illustrated Directory of Architects*. Partners or chief officers of the firms concerned should be interviewed and particularly senior members of the staff who will be directly responsible for the work. It is important (though rarely done) to visit some of the recent jobs of the firm, and to enquire of the occupants or the owners as to the successes and failures of the work. There are significant percentages of variation between the performance of different firms and of various methods of contract, and the client has a responsibility, not only to himself, but to his organization, to obtain sufficient quality and the best value for money.

Feasibility studies may be commissioned for particular sites or buildings for which the professional team will make a separate charge. These should be negotiated in advance for delivery within an agreed time. Such reports often throw up a number of subsidiary problems concerning, for example, geological site conditions, drainage, planning restrictions, highway improvement lines, accessibility, etc. Each one of these may require other detailed investigations by particular experts. It is obvious that to skimp the cost and consequent depth of such investigations may be to put at risk, unnecessarily, the control of the cost and the length of time the building takes to be constructed.

The key decisions made by the client at the outset have a major effect upon the way building is managed and constructed on the site, and upon the time it takes, and money it costs. So it is necessary to set out at this point some of the key factors.

Forms of contract

Figures 3.1 to 3.6 analyse the characteristics of most of the available varieties of contract. Note the weaknesses shown in many of them where the necessary supply of information does not bear parallel legal responsibility.

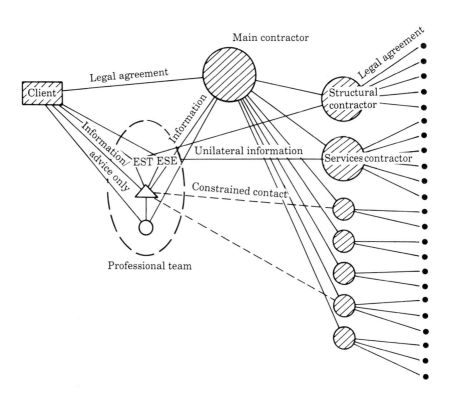

Figure 3.1 *The lump sum contract.*

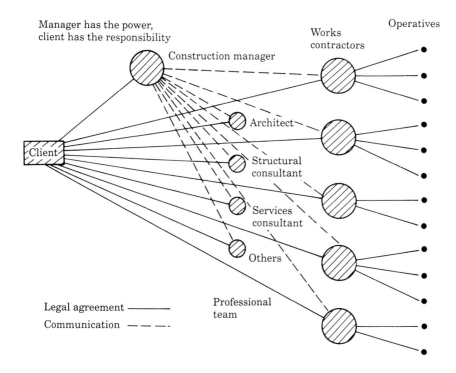

Figure 3.2 *The construction management contract.*

Plan of work

The plan of work (Table 3.1) shows the various stages through which an orthodox building scheme proceeds. The precise form depends upon the type of contract and the character of the professional and construction firms involved. This in turn will depend upon the nature of the work itself. For instance, if the building is a fairly standard one, such as a group of houses, a standard factory, or a regular office block, where the ground conditions are known and there are no unusual problems concerning services or adjacent buildings, then there are unlikely to be significant areas of unknowns. So long as there is sufficient time then proper drawings and specifications can be prepared and checked, bills of quantities or basic schedule of quantified items (BSQI) can be built up and the scheme go to tender. If this work is professionally and competently done, then

Table 3.1 Outline plan of work
(Taken from the full version by the Royal Institute of British Architects)
A general picture of the building process

Preliminary services

Stage	Purpose of work and decisions to be reached	Tasks to be done	People directly involved	Usual terminology
A Inception	To prepare general outline of requirements and plan future action.	Set up client organization for briefing. Consider requirements, appoint architect.	All client interests, architect	Briefing
B Feasibility	To provide the client with an appraisal and recommendation in order that he may determine the form in which the project is to proceed, ensuring that it is feasible, functionally, technically and financially.	Carry out studies of user requirements, site conditions, planning, design, and cost, etc., as necessary to reach decisions.	Clients' representatives, architects, engineers, and QS according to nature of project.	

Basic services

C Outline proposals	To determine general approach to layout, design and construction in order to obtain authoritative approval of the client on the outline proposals and accompanying report.	Develop the brief further. Carry out studies on user requirements, technical problems, planning, design and costs, as necessary to reach decisions.	All client interests, architects, engineers, QS and specialists as required.	Sketch plans

Stage	Purpose	Description	People involved	
D Scheme design	To complete the brief and decide on particular proposals, including planning arrangement appearance, constructional method, outline specification, and cost, and to obtain all approvals.	Final development of the brief, full design of the project by architect, preliminary design by engineers, preparation of cost plan and full explanatory report. Submission of proposals for all approvals.	All client interests, architects, engineers, QS and specialists and all statutory and other approving authorities.	Working drawings

Brief should not be modified after this point

Stage	Purpose	Description	People involved
E Detail design	To obtain final decision on every matter related to design, specification, construction and cost.	Full design of every part and component of the building by collaboration of all concerned. Complete cost checking of designs.	Architects, QS, engineers and specialists, contractor (if appointed)

Any further change in location, size, shape, or cost after this time will result in abortive work

Stage	Purpose	Description	People involved
F Production information	To prepare production information and make final detailed decisions to carry out work.	Preparation of final production information i.e. drawings, schedules and specifications.	Architects, engineers and specialists, contractor (if appointed).
G Bills of Quantities	To prepare and complete all information and arrangements for obtaining tender.	Preparations of Bills of Quantities and tender documents	Architects, QS, contractor (if appointed)
H Tender action	Action as recommended in NJCC *Code of Procedure for Selective Tendering 1972.***	Action as recommended in NJCC *Code of Procedure for Selective Tendering 1972.***	Architects, QS, engineers, contractor, client.

Table 3.1, cont.

Any further change in location, size, shape, or cost after this time will result in abortive work

Stage	Purpose of work and decisions to be reached	Tasks to be done	People directly involved	Usual terminology
J Project planning	To enable the contractor to programme the work in accordance with contract conditions; brief site inspectorate, and make arrangements to commence work on site.	Action in accordance with *The Management of Building Contracts*** and Diagram 9.	Contractor, sub-contractors.	Site operations
K Operations on site	To follow plans through to practical completion of the building	Action in accordance with *The Management of Building Contracts*** and Diagram 10.	Architects, engineers, contractors, sub-contractors, QS, client.	
L Completion	To hand over the building to the client for occupation, remedy and defects, settle the final account, and complete all work in accordance with the contract.	Action in accordance with *The Management of Building Contracts* and Diagram 11.	Architects, engineers, contractor, QS, client.	
M Feed-back	To analyse the management, construction and performance of the project.	Analysis of job records. Inspection of completed building. Studies of building in use.	Architect, engineers, QS, contractor, client.	

* from the RIBA *Plan of Work*.
** The publications *Code of Procedure for Selective Tendering* (NJCC 1972) and *The Management of Building Contracts* (NJCC 1970) are published by RIBA Publications Ltd for the NJCC.

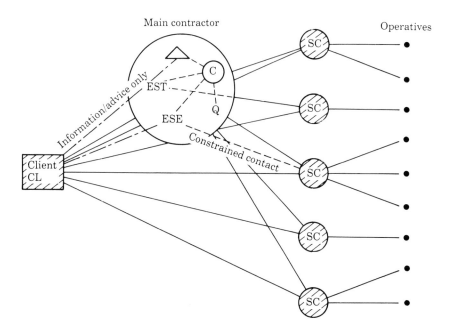

Figure 3.3 *The management fee contract.*

the tender prices coming in should be reasonably close to the original estimates and, so long as reputable contractors are employed, it is likely that the scheme will be built to time and to price. However, surprisingly few buildings nowadays are regular repeats. Clients are tempted to go for longer tender lists and competition to win is acute. This in turn can produce problems which induce many contractors to read the small print of the standard form of contract and to employ claims surveyors to find every available opportunity for claiming extra payments. This makes the period of preparation of critical importance, most particularly in the orthodox method.

Though the earlier stages of the plan of work will be more or less identical for whichever method of organization is used, the relationship of the professional and construction firms, together with the form of contract, will have a major effect upon the way the site is managed (Figure 3.6). The following are some of the alternatives:

1. Competitive tender

This is the orthodox method used in the building industry in this country. As will be seen from the plan of work, the drawings, specifications and schedules culminate in the preparation of the bills of quantities by the quantity surveyor. This document is primarily for the purposes of obtaining tenders from different contractors for precisely the same quantum and quality of work. It is clear that any tendering process that has more than one variable is much more difficult to assess properly. For instance, it is much more difficult to judge a scheme where, say, a design is submitted in conjunction with the price. For out of six designs one may be the best, but the price may be unacceptable, or vice versa. Such a situation has, theoretically, a number of variables and is difficult to judge fairly. It is therefore better to obtain prices upon the basis of a good design which has been properly measured so that the resulting tender prices are strictly comparable.

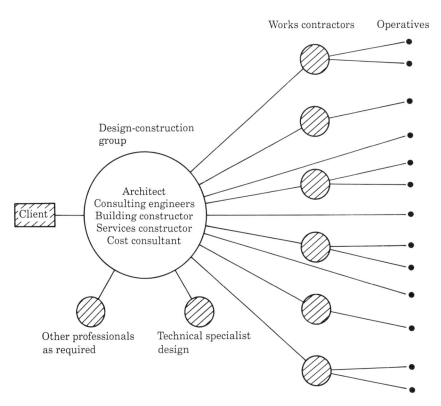

Figure 3.4 *The design-construction group contract.*

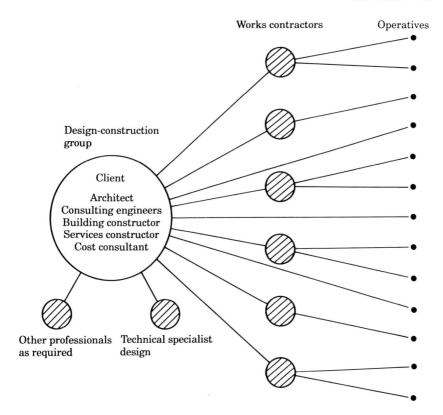

Figure 3.5 *The design-construction group contract with client participation.*

2. *Negotiation (Schedule of Rates)*

This is where the architect and/or quantity surveyor, on the client's behalf, negotiate the price for a particular scheme by means of schedule of rates. This method may be satisfactory if it is part of the continuum of work with the same contractor. It is a method which cannot be used indefinitely because prices have, in the end, to be related to the trend in the market if the client is to get a fair deal.

3. *Package deal with bills of quantities*

A number of contractors are keen to offer schemes and bids. In this situation a client is offered the services of an in-house architect and engineers' department, or alternatively an out-of-house private firm employed by the contractor. Clients should be aware that such firms owe a fiduciary (unbiased) service, not to the client, but to the contractor, and if and when the going gets rough this is to the clients' disadvantage. If a number of package deal contractors offer schemes to the same client for the same job, then the contractors have to bear a larger overhead to cover the cost of preparing unsuccessful schemes. In the package deal boom of the early '60s one national contractor reported that he prepared 31 schemes for

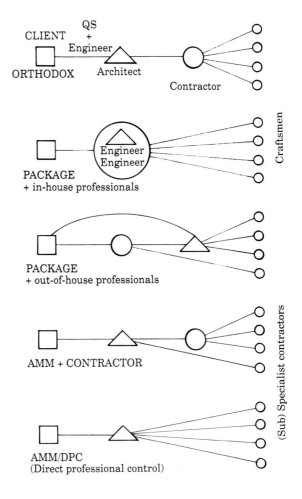

Figure 3.6 *Relationships in various forms of contract.*

every successful one executed. It will be appreciated that the overhead cost of all this unsuccessful work was out of proportion to the profit gained by him for the one successful job. Hence many national contractors closed their package deal departments down. At the time of writing another package deal boom is starting and will no doubt end in the same way. Clients should not feel, as many do, that somehow they can get the design work for nothing. Design input, both architectural and engineering, is expensive to prepare if it is done properly by skilled people, and will be paid for by the client. It is better for him that the cost of it should be known in the open, rather than concealed and covered by the general cost of building.

4. *Architectural competition*

There is a growing interest in the use of architectural competition, especially for public sector work. This has a number of advantages from the community's point of view, but takes some skill and understanding to operate effectively. It may be noted that in Germany architectural competitions are commonplace and the resulting much higher standard of architecture is a tangible benefit to that nation. However, the process takes a fair amount of time, the assessors have to be paid, and it is usual to offer consolation prizes to the second and third runners-up. In the end the client gets the best possible architectural result so long as the competition brief has been carefully and expertly written. This is of the greatest importance.

The client may be represented on the assessors' jury and he also has the power to choose the expert members of that body. The rules for competitions are laid down by an international agreement and are available from the RIBA. If the standard form of competition does not appeal, maybe the 'promoters choice' type of competition could be a satisfactory form. In this case, three firms may be shortlisted and the client can then visit each in turn to satisfy himself which one would be the most expert and able to carry out the scheme.

The most important thing by far in the running of successful competitions is the very careful and thorough brief writing by the assessors. The French and the Germans can be particularly good at this but in the last few decades the British have become rather sloppy and disorganized. It is no good undertaking the important work of promoting a competition unless very experienced and expert people are used, particularly at the brief writing stage. It is then of paramount importance to stick to the rules. For instance there has recently been a very large design and bid competition organized by a nationalized undertaking for a large tract of land in West London. The rules were not professionally written and the promoters declared that, in the second stage when the designs and tenders had been submitted, the best scheme would win. However, when it came to the point, the scheme which obeyed the brief was not supported by the lowest tender. The promoters then changed their minds and started, what in effect, became a Dutch auction. Had the entrants known that this was going to happen at the end of the competition they would not have wasted their time and effort. In this particular instance the winning design was seen by all the other competitors who were then given a chance by the promoter to 'improve' their design. That was rather like playing poker when everyone could see your hand. The National Gallery competition was another example of promoters changing their minds during the course of the competition, the assessors judgement being bypassed. A case of mismanagement.

Clients have sometimes criticized the competition system on the basis that the production of many unsuccessful schemes means that big overheads for redundant work have to be charged out on the few successful schemes. This is an inaccurate picture for it is customary for some architects to do the occasional competition in their spare time. If they did not do so, they would eventually be bankrupted.

5. *Management contract*

This method has been pioneered by Bovis and the form has been taken up by a number of other major contractors. In this case the management contractors offer themselves as agents of the clients and for a fee obtain tenders from the trade contractors and suppliers required to erect the building. The client may feel more vulnerable in that he is patently taking the risk as compared with the orthodox competitive tender procedure described above. However, as has been stated before, the JCT Forms of Contract absolve the contractor from much of the responsibility which is put back onto the shoulders of the client. And so it can be said that there is not much real difference in the responsibility the client carries with the management form of contract. One obtains the skill in buying and management of an experienced team, and all the prices and measurements are open. The method can become bureaucratic and some professional firms report that this increases their own internal costs significantly. If one is fortunate in having a good team for a particular project, then it can be a satisfactory procedure. It has one disadvantage in terms of principle, – that is that it adds one more link in the chain of communication (Figure 2.1). Where professional firms of architects/engineers cannot be found to undertake the construction management role, then the management contractor fulfils a need. It is a matter of trusting the contractor.

Project Management

In the USA, many of the leading firms of architects/engineers have a 'construction management' department. This is the basis of their CM approach and by-and-large it works well. The departments are well integrated and do not add another unnecessary link in the vital communications chain between design team and client because they are in effect part of the design team.

However, in both the USA and in the UK, there are also independent firms of project managers. They purport to 'act as the client for the client' and come between the real client and the design team, thus forming an extra link in the communications chain between the design team and the real client. For an additional fee the project managers may be given the responsibility of engaging the various members of the design team, and then to brief them, oversee their performance, authorize fees, approve design team instructions, etc.

What tends to happen in such circumstances is that the project management firm passes its legal responsibilities on to the shoulders of the design team, whilst retaining the power to control. There have been a number of unhappy failures of jobs as a result of this flawed system. Such jobs will work tolerably if the project management firm operates in the spirit of the conditions of engagement, but as soon as a less experienced member of the project management firm starts operating jobs by the letter of the conditions, the situation deteriorates dangerously.

A recent example will make the point. A teaching hospital in a rambling old collection of buildings engaged an independent project manager for a complex rehabilitation job. A leading firm of experienced hospital architects were engaged and prepared a good scheme. The form of contract was chosen by the project management firm. Various key parts of the building could not be surveyed properly, because the building was occupied and working. As soon as suspended ceilings were removed and ducts opened up, the original survey assumptions were found to be wrong. This made it necessary for the design team to issue a large number of architect's instructions so that the contractors could proceed without expensive delay. The project management firm declined to approve a majority of architect's instructions, leaving the design team responsible in law for the value of the varied work. In the event the job overran seriously on both cost and time. As a consequence morale was seriously affected to the detriment of service to the client. In addition to this a large quantity of unnecessary paperwork was generated, most of it defensive.

Firms of engineers report that independent project management firms cause them about double the paperwork and they need to charge extra fees for the additional work. One such firm reports a six times increase in paperwork on another hospital job in London. So the message is: do not employ independent project managers who purport to know everything about building. The design team, if chosen well, will know much more about building than any single project manager.

If the client body is too busy and needs support, the logical answer is to get someone who has had a great deal of experience within the client's organization and who thus can interpret it to the design team direct. There is no need for amateur building managers in that position.

The USA style of facilitative project management can be

valuable. This style keeps the project manager outside the design and construction teams and the client's organization; in fact it is his independence which enhances the trust he generates. He regards his job as that of keeping the objectives to the fore in everyone's mind, talking straight to the teams and to the client, keeping a practised eye on the cost, construction, quality and programme strategies, and sorting out personal incompatibilities. He is the antithesis of the 'pig-in-the-middle' issuing forms and adjudicating change-orders, rather he discourages backside protective paperwork.

6. *Direct professional control or Advanced Method of Management (AMM)*

This is a method which is used almost universally in the German construction industry and is now growing strongly in the United States where it is known as Construction Management (CM). It is the method which used to be employed in the great age of high quality building in this country in the 17th and 18th Centuries, and is now being revived here. It involves the de-isolation of the professional team from their comparatively isolated offices and their establishment full time on site at the construction stage. As with management contracting, the team working on behalf of the client obtains best-buy tenders from the trade contractors and suppliers concerned in the erection of the building. It is an open book operation wherein each of the trade contractors signs a contract direct with the client, so the client signs a number of contracts for the total job instead of just one. The on-site professional team have the responsibility of co-ordinating the work of the trade contractors and can be sued if they do not perform. This method has the advantage that the number of possible breakdowns in communication are reduced to a minimum (Figure 2.2). The designers of the building and its consequent engineering, who know every detail and every reason for the myriad of decisions made in the drawings and documents are consequently the best people to direct the physical interpretation on site. The method assumes that the professional on-site team is thoroughly conversant with construction methods and has the confidence and experience to programme and manage the trade contractors. It means also that the designers can keep a strict eye on the performance of the trade contractors and can duplicate firms or, if necessary, terminate unilaterally those who perform badly or late. This is a powerful positive weapon in the proper maintenance of the programme and the achievement of the completion date. This compares favourably with the orthodox procedures, where the professional team has no power to rectify the programme or quality that is going wrong. The only course left under such circumstances is to sue for damages after the event. With DPC (AMM) it is helpful if the quantity surveyor has also measured out the estimated labour times for each of the operations, as in the Examples in Chapter 4. This enables the team to prepare a labour loading graph from which the day to day control of the job can be administered and up-dated.

This emerging method does depend upon the client taking the risk and being able to identify and appoint professional teams competent to perform in this way. There are a number of firms of architects and engineers who want to be involved in the actual making of the buildings they have designed and detailed.

The Building Research Establishment has produced a graph (Figure 3.7) comparing an AMM job to Crown contracts. The AMM job was both quicker and more economical than conventional run jobs. The graph was not given wide publicity on the basis that 'One swallow does not a summer make', in other words, one sample is not statistically significant. Since then there have been many AMM jobs run by practices specializing in this work which exhibit a similar success ratio.

Bonds

The client may still feel, as with management contracting, that he is vulnerable. However, in practical fact, once again, the let-out clauses in the JCT form of contract mean that he is really no more vulnerable with this method than he is with the orthodox contract. Nevertheless, he may wish to purchase additional assurance in cases where public accountability is a major factor. This involves each of the trade contractors, suppliers, plus the professional team, providing assurance bonds, co-ordinated into one package for the total contract. This adds to the cost.

The sum of the trade contractors and suppliers, together with

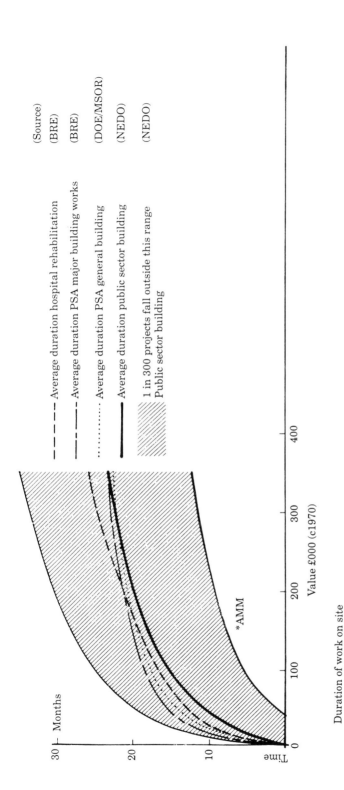

Figure 3.7 *The Building Research Establishment has found that one AMM contract was more economical and quicker than other conventionally-run Crown contracts.*

the preliminary costs and the normal professional fees, are the same for both the orthodox and DPC (AMM). In the case of the orthodox method, the main contractor adds his head-office overheads and profit. This compares with DPC (AMM) where the additional project management fee which may be less. If assurance is necessary, then the cost of this will have to be added, and this may amount to 1–5% extra. The client then has to weigh up whether the let-out clauses in the JCT form of contract are more of a risk to him than the fiduciary service of the professional management team with, or without its assurance cover.

Motive

The quality of architecture, that is for efficiency, economy, delight, depends upon the calibre of the architect. In the same way, the efficiency of construction, control of cost, the mastery of the time programme, and the maintenance of a consistent and appropriate quality depends upon the calibre of site manage-ment *coupled with their aims.* If the management teams are in line with your aims, then it is more likely you will have a satisfactory job. If their aims differ in any important respect, i.e. if they want to maximize their profits at your expense, then it is necessary to be very much on your guard. A client accustomed to procuring building programmes has to react to defects in the system.

Incidentally, there are many variations of the broad groupings described above, but it is not appropriate in this book to go into them because, generally speaking, they do not affect the actual process of site management significantly. There are no real short cuts to the critical decisions the client must take in selecting the best possible team. The problem of selecting the best architect has been referred to above. He in turn will recommend the appointment of a quantity surveyor or cost consultant if the job is large enough, and of the structural and services engineers. If a multi-professional firm is selected then these disciplines may already be incorporated in the professional firm. It may be galling to the client to have to take on board so many separate professional firms in the former case. Nevertheless, as with the choice of architect, so with the choice of the other professional members of the ad hoc team there are horses for courses. A firm of structural engineers may be very skilled in dealing with only a few types of structure, others may be more appropriate in the particular case the client has in mind. The architect may have had better experience with a particular firm and would prefer to work with them. Firms vary in quality between the partners, both in terms of compatibility and of experience. Firms have varying pressures of work and availability of the right level of staffing. The size of a firm is an important consideration. Large firms in general find it more difficult to tackle small jobs satisfactorily. One may need a particular partner to tackle ones own special job. Quite often a firm is appointed with a particular partner in mind. If the work is subsequently delegated to someone else, this can cause disappointment and disillusion.

Client involvement – After Scheme Approval

Once the client has approved the scheme design and the quantity surveyor's estimate of the total cost, he will be called upon from time to time to choose between alternatives and their costs relating to equipment finishes and fittings.

Any alterations to the character or content of the scheme is likely to involve abortive work and raise the spectre of claims for extra fees from the professional team. If, however, the production drawing and estimating plan has been drawn up in such a way to allow tranches of money for special equipment, fittings and finishes etc., then, so long as the client's own work being done in parallel conforms to the budget ceiling, all should be well. It is therefore wise at the stage when production drawings start to make clear those areas which should be left for later detailing in line with the client's own development work.

Specialist items

Unfortunately main contractors do not like the device of the prime cost sum which is the conventional way of dealing with specialist items. Most architects feel that this is an essential tool, allowing them to nominate contractors and/or suppliers whom they are sure will provide the right sort of specialist work and upon whom they can rely. Contractors complain that nominated specialist contractors covered by such PC (Prime Cost) sums can hold them to ransom and not agree to the contractor's programme or to the small print of the sub-contract form. If the specialist firm or supplier is mentioned in the contract documents at the time of tender, then there is no real excuse for a main contractor to claim extras for any difficulties and consequent disruption to programme, because he can reassure himself about the willingness of the specialist contractor to comply and can make allowance for this in his tender. However, if specialist contractors or suppliers are nominated *after* tender the contractor should have the right to object. (This facility is provided in the ACA Contract.) Complaints from contractors about nominated sub-contractors can occasionally be a claims device.

Comprehensive definition

Where the JCT '63 or '80 form of contract is used, it is essential for the entire building to be completely visualized and detailed, all the equipment decided upon and finishes agreed, every detail drawn and precisely described in the bills of quantity, several months before work commences on site. For regular jobs which are virtually repeats of previous buildings and where no departures are made in terms of constructional method, services or finishing techniques, then this is possible to achieve. For fear of claims, everything must be drawn and described. As has been stated previously a proportion of the drawings produced for the average job of this sort are in fact redundant. Were the contractor willing to execute the building in accordance with the general architectural intentions of the drawings, then far fewer would be necessary, and with good craftsmen the result would be just as good. The difference represents part of the claims potential of the job.

An architect commissioned by a builders' property company finds that far fewer drawings are called for and there is no claims hassle.

Limited number of drawings

A new form of contract has been developed by the ACA which opens up new possibilities on these lines. In one alternative clause provision is made for the architect who produces a finite number of drawings which illustrate those parts of the building which require positive control. Thereafter it is laid upon the contractor to furnish any such additional drawings he may find necessary, at his own expense and to the approval of the architect and the client. This is a technique currently used in the United States. One snag is that alterations made after tender can be expensive.

It should be emphasized that alterations are costly for the contractor perhaps more than the face value of the remeasured work in terms of the disruption of his organization and the co-ordination of the trade contractors and suppliers concerned. The very fact that operatives have to be laid off or transferred to other jobs means that others will have to relearn what the laid-off operatives already know. It is seldom that the same men are available at the precise time when the work restarts. Deliveries have to be arrested or materials have to be housed for longer periods. All manner of other difficulties can occur. So with an orthodox contract it is important to use ones best endeavours to produce a completely detailed scheme during the production drawing stage and before the drawings are sent to the quantity surveyor for the preparation of the bills of quantities.

Schemes not completely detailed

There are types of scheme where it is not possible to make final decisions about all parts at an early stage. The main contractor or the tendering contractors, at tender stage, must then be required to allow for decisions to be made for parts of the job at a later stage and their prices can then include for this. Where the client has development work of his own to co-ordinate with the building programme, – for instance special foundation bases for new machines or special services, or air conditioning for electronic equipment, or furniture and fittings which cannot be decided upon until the occupancy has been determined – then it is as well for the form of contract to allow the architect, on behalf of the client, to have a direct relationship with the trade contractors rather than to be cut off from them through the interposition of a main contractor. In such cases the client may choose a management contract of the Bovis type, or the Direct Professional Control (AMM) type. This type of environment means, of necessity, that the client will be much involved in the details of the work on the production drawings and later in the management process on site.

Line of authorization

It is then necessary for the client to appoint a director or a senior person to be the principal through whom communication and decision is channelled. He *must* have the writ of his committee or board of directors to make decisions of an appropriate scale without delay. It is of critical importance that, under no circumstances is he bypassed, say to the chairman of the board or, in the other direction, by managers or directors of departments directly to the professional team, or to the trade contractors. The principal should communicate solely through the nominated partner of the professional team. It is most helpful if he can attend professional team meetings during the production drawing stage, at the site mobilization meetings, and at the site management meetings. In this way he is kept completely in the picture and will have an in-depth understanding of all the processes going on. This will make him an invaluable interpreter of these events to his own people.

Short circuits

There are ways in which this important point can be misinterpreted, – one example may suffice: an office block in the City of London had to be modified to take a large computer. It was a rapid building job which had to be done in eleven weeks.

At the weekly site meetings, many of those attending came from various departments of the client's institution. During the course of the work they had agreed to various amendments and additions which affected the budget. Although all this had been fully reported in the minutes of the meetings, neither the chief engineer nor his board members either received reports from those attending the site meetings, or read the minutes. Consequently they were surprised by the amount of the final account. From this example it can be seen that unless the client's representative is senior enough and has sufficient confidence to report the full consequences of decisions made by the site team, with his approval, then things can go wrong. It can be seen also from this example that if the client's representative has to refer back and delay decisions, this can have very expensive consequences, especially with a rapid building programme.

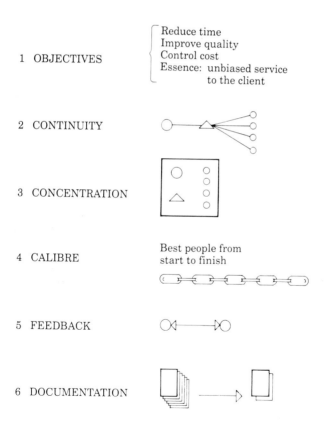

Figure 3.8 *Six principles.*

The client function analysed

The following is an analysis of the client function taken from the RIBA Plan of Work with comments: (The original numbering has not been maintained.) See also *An Architects Guide to Fee Negotiations* by Ray Moxley.

Stage A – Inception

1 Consider the need to build.
2 Set up an organization with a chairman to manage the matter from the client end, e.g. committee or working party, departmental representatives, secretary, decision making machinery, liaison representation for design team, etc.
3 Appoint architect.
4 Commence exchange with architect and note and act on architect's opinion and advice.
5 Discuss terms of appointment of consultants.
6 Appoint remainder of design team for Stage B as advised by the architect.

During this stage the architect is obtaining background information, meeting the client, telling him about the professional role, receiving instructions, and undertaking further researches that may be necessary, considering a programme for the professional work, obtaining OS maps, making an initial site visit and making enquiries about QSs and engineers.

Stage B – Feasibility

1 Contribute to design team meeting.
   The agenda for this meeting will state objectives, outline requirements, completion time and costs, will give information about the site. It will determine priorities and deal with methods of communication.
2 Provide all information required by the architect. Assist as

required in studies carried out by design team. If necessary, initiate and conclude according to time-table, studies within own organization. Make decisions on all matters submitted for decision relevant to Stage B. The architect will be preparing studies and will initiate other studies by consultants as required. He will report to the client on feasibility of the project and make recommendations. During this time he will study the site and local information, initiate enquiries with the local authorities and other bodies. He will prepare design work necessary to establish with the quanitity surveyor the general feasibility of the project. The structural engineers and the mechanical and electrical engineers will do the work necessary to help the architect in preparing a practical scheme.

3 Receive feasibility report, discuss and consider.
4 Decide to abandon, modify, or proceed with project. Instruct architect accordingly.
5 Confirm existing appointments: appoint further consultants as recommended by architect.
6 Agree timetable, working method for subsequent stages, tender procedure and contract arrangements. The architect now has a timetable of working methods, tender procedures and contract arrangements.

Stage C – Outline proposals

1 Contribute to meeting
  This meeting with the professional team has the following agenda: brief, site plans and other site data, cost limits based on the client's brief, timetable and dimensional methods. It determines priorities, defines roles and responsibilities and deals with communication methods. It sets out the tender procedures and contract arrangements, agrees on systems of costs and engineering checks, the type of bill of quantities or basic schedule of quantified items (BSQI) and a list of actions to be taken together with programming and progressing techniques.
2 Provide all information required by architect. Assist as required in studies carried out by the design team. If necessary, initiate and conclude studies within his own organization according to the timetable. Make decisions on all matters relevant to Stage D submitted for decision.

During this stage the architect will complete the user studies, develop the detailed planning solutions, consult other members of the team on the results of their work, prepare a full scheme design taking individual and group advice, pass the scheme drawings to the QS for him to prepare a draft cost plan on the basis of the scheme design together with statements of quality, standards and functional requirements. The engineers will make design sketches and calculations to define the full scheme will go as far as section, sizes and materials, foundations, drain runs, etc. The services engineers will finalize the mechanical and electrical scheme design including a form of lighting, heating and air distribution. The architect will receive the engineers' proposals and review the scheme, and design and modify as necessary. With the engineers and QS he will prepare the final cost plan and the outline specification. These will be presented in report form with drawings to the client.

3 Receive scheme and report from the architect, conclude, according to timetable, any studies that are required within own organizations.

During this period the architect deals with questionnaires, discussions, visits, observations, users' studies, etc., and initaties studies by consultants as the client requires. He has a general role of co-ordination. He analyses similar projects if necessary, provides a study of circulation space and other similar problems, tries a number of planning solutions, and in co-operation with the quantity surveyor and engineers, tries out various structural and environmental solutions best suited to the evolving scheme. During this time the quantity surveyor helps with various cost studies of the details. The structural and services engineers study alternative methods and make comparisons.

4 Receive architect's report; consider, discuss and decide outstanding issues. Give instructions for further action. The outline planning application is then submitted by the architect to the planning authority, after consultation.

The safest way to deal with official approvals from the point of view of both building regulations and planning permission is to put these operations end to end. This takes a great deal of time and many firms now elide as many procedures as possible. It is usually not possible to elide the stage of final planning permission unless the client is prepared to take a risk and has done the necessary research with the planning authority to be sure that his development has undoubted support. (Figure 3.9).

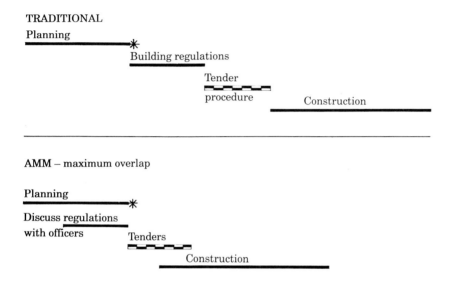

Figure 3.9 *Dealing with approvals.*

Stage D – Scheme design

1 Contribute to next meeting.
2 The agenda will include a review of progress, firming up of the brief, consideration of priorities and a detailed discussion of the architect's report tabled. Give full consideration, discuss, make views known and make decisions.
3 Approve scheme.
4 Note future programme and take all appropriate action on site acquisition, reorganization, plant ordering, etc.
5 Note necessity to freeze ideas at this point. This is the last time that the brief can be modified.

Stage E – Detailed design

At this stage the architect organizes the design team and incorporates the client's final decisions on the brief. With the team's assistance he establishes roles and responsibilities, prepares the plan of work and a timetable.

1 Provide any final information required by architect.
2 Decide all matters put up for decision.
   During this stage the architect will carry out the detailed design in accordance with the programme in close collaboration with the engineers and QS who will carry out immediate cost checks. All the members of the design team will be kept up to date by him and he will be receiving at this time the engineers' and other specialist drawings which will be co-ordinated into the drawings and checked by the QS for the cost plan. He will then call a meeting of the design team to reconcile, as necessary, the developing information. No further changes will be made after this time to size, shape, location or cost. The engineers will now be carrying out their design work in accordance with the agreed proposals. Any further change in size, location, shape or cost after this time will result in abortive work and extra cost.
   Detail planning application is then submitted to the planning authority by the architect. Bye-law/building act approvals are sought after consultation.

Stage F – Production information

The object of this stage is to prepare the working drawings (production information) in every particular so that the trade contractors of all the trades can complete the work. Depending upon the type of contract used and the nature of the drawing programme some of the details can be left to the later stages as have been described elsewhere. Stage F normally sees the bulk of the production information being prepared. This may be in the form of drawings, schedules and specifications and it involves the architects, structural engineers, services engineers and any specialist contractors whose work needs to be drawn, described or specified so that it can be co-ordinated with all the general detailing work.

Stage G – Bills of Quantities

During this period the quantity surveyor will receive from the architect all the material necessary to prepare the bill of quantities for the job. This is a lengthy, detailed document which measures all the labour and materials which go together to make the job and forms a standard basis upon which tenders may be received. It saves each of the tendering contractors preparing his own measurements of the job and makes sure that they all tender on the same basis. Theoretically the client only pays, therefore, for one bill of quantities rather than six or however many tenderers there are. During this time the architect recommends a short list of tenderers and obtains the client's agreement. It may well be possible to rationalize this process and save time by opening negotiations with reliable trade contractors who can abbreviate standard methods. The client should be consulted and advised of the risks.

Stage H – Tender action

There is a code of procedure for selective tendering which briefly concerns the technique for issuing and receiving tenders, the opening of tenders and the selection of the successful contractor and the notification of those who are unsuccessful.

Stage J – Project planning

1 Make the necessary financial arrangements to deal with monthly certificates for payment.
   The architect will tell the client about the responsibilities of administering the contract and the financial arrangements suitable for the job.
2 Check contract documents and sign them. Make the necessary insurance arrangements.

3 Contribute to the mobilization meeting.
4 Prepare to hand over the site to the contractor.
   The architect sets out the procedures for the contract and
   its administration, makes suitable financial arrangements
   and agrees methods of communication. He will prepare sets
   of contract documents for the contractor, together with
   production information, brief site staff and nominate sub-
   contractors, if this has not already been done. He will hold the
   first project meeting. The contractor will check the contract
   documents, sign them, appoint site staff and make reserva-
   tions for early plant requirements, deal with insurance and
   undertake the pre-contract planning, make arrangements
   with sub-contractors and deal with the mobilization problems
   concerning stores, site huts, security, etc.

Stage K – Operations on Site

1 Hand over the site to the contractor.
2 Honour certificates within the period stated within the
  contract.
3 Note progress and financial statements and approve justified
  increase costs.
4 Witness M & E acceptance tests if desired.
5 Appoint operating and maintenance staff in good time.

During this time the architect has a number of management jobs
to perform but the burden of the work falls upon the contractor
and the principal trade contractors. The architect and the
engineers provide detailed information, and check that the
quality of the work built is generally up to the standard they
have drawn and specified in the contract documents at the
relevant stages of the programme. The QS will be valuing work
and materials on site, and preparing certificates for regular
payment.

Stage L – Completion

1 Arrange insurance.
2 Attend meeting and take over building for occupation.

3 Honour certificates.
4 Report defects which require immediate attention as they occur.
5 Contribute to feedback reviews.

During this period the architect will make a thorough practical completion inspection and if the building or the section of the building being considered is safe and can be used without undue inconvenience, by the client, he will sign a practical completion certificate which will have the consequence of requiring the building owner to release a half of the retention fund. The engineers will be involved in inspecting the structure and the services engineers will be involved in inspecting the proper functioning of mechanical services. The contractor will be notified of what items will need attention and he will be given the opportunity to rectify these.

6 Collaborate in the architect's pre-final inspection.
7 Agree programme for remedial work.
8 Collaborate in final inspection.
9 Honour certificates if issued.
10 Honour final certificate.

At the end of the defects liability period which is normally six months from practical completion, the building is finally inspected to make sure all the faults are rectified. In the case of services the period must include a heating and/or cooling season. The final inspection of the works involves the issuing of a certificate of making good defects and the release of the residue of the retention fund. The QS deals with the final account and the final certificate is issued.

Diminishing role of the client in the orthodox method

It will be seen from the foregoing that the client is in the hands of the professional team as soon as the brief has been firmed up. Indeed, the architect can often have a large hand in preparing the brief. It is as well that this should be so, because he can often open up possibilities in, say, materials, or spans of structure, of which the client may not have been aware. Too tight a brief can be wastefully inhibiting and too broad a brief may miss the essence of the client's needs and thus require wasteful repetition of the scheme design stage.

Continuing client involvement

Where there are areas of unknowns at contract stage then the cost plan will have tranches of money allowed for the unknown or undefined items. The professional team should prepare a programme of freeze dates for information before which detailed information about these areas must be settled in time for the professional team to prepare the drawings and go through the tender procedure to select the best trade contractors and suppliers to suit the work. This integration does mean that the professional team must have control of the trade contractors and the inter-related programme, and thus, the management contract or DPC (AMM) contract are the most likely types of contract to be chosen. In these instances the client's involvement is continuous through his nominated director or senior representative, who should attend the meetings and authorize and approve the way the information is crystallized out in detail.

Planned building economics

There is a great deal of continuing experience within the building industry held by competent quantity surveyors on the cost of all manner of building processes, not only in terms of geography – for every part of the country has different building cost characteristics – but also in terms of types of buildings under various conditions. It is not a difficult matter for such a quantity surveyor to allow fair and reasonable sums for the inclusion of a wide variety of work at later stages in the contract. It is of course, sound business practice to confirm these budget figures by actually going to tender to groups of trade contractors or trade suppliers, reasonably close to the time when the work will be required and bearing in mind known delivery lead times.

There are benefits to be derived from this process in that trade contractors do not have to cover themselves prematurely against inflation, about which the quantity surveyor, with his wider perspective, will often have a more reliable view. Furthermore, the trade contractor or supplier can be given more precise operational dates and thus be in a better position to see what his labour force is likely to be at the critical time. This will enable him to estimate more closely.

Some enlightened clients are now asking for 'cost-in-use' studies to be prepared at an early stage for, say, a thirty year period. The cost consultant then estimates the anticipated life of each element of the fabric, the services, the external works and the finishes. The figures are usually based on present-day prices. The cost of repair and replacement is, at the time of writing, not subject to tax, (though it can be to VAT), whereas the capital cost of building is. So high quality building for long life is penalized by the Inland Revenue. The client has to bear this in mind when comparing the extra cost better materials and equipment with the potential saving in repairs and replacements over the years.

Clairvoyance

The orthodox procedures, where everything must be cut and dried many months before work starts on site, do require the architect and his professional colleagues to exercise a degree of clairvoyance, about the detailed nature of the building, which is beyond normal human capacity. In parallel with the professional team's imaginative exercises interpreted into drawings, the client has to learn the nature of the building from the descriptions and the drawings. The client is most often surprised to see the physical form as it emerges on site and it is often the case that he desperately wants to make better use of the accommodation when he at last realizes its true nature. Alas, he does not have the benefit of the architect and his professional colleagues' training in three-dimensional imagination and it would be unfair to expect him to be able to make up his mind at such an early stage. The system of information freeze dates, realistically related to the lead times for the supply and erection of the various stages of the building work, is better related to the client's operational needs.

The Client's Role in more detail with a Management Contract or DPC (AMM)

The clearer the idea that the client has about his needs the greater the degree of certainty that the architect will develop about the size and shape of the building and its contents, and the closer the QS will get in his estimate to the final cost of the building.

Let us assume for the purpose of the following description that tranches of money have been allowed for air conditioning, terminal equipment in laboratories, built-in furniture in board room and committee room, carpets and soft furnishings, shop fitting for retail units, special conveyors, the rehabilitation of and alteration of an existing building. It would clearly be a waste of valuable time if the whole contract was held up because decisions could not be made on these items. The QS is able to allow tranches of money which will be close in practical terms to what is required, assuming certain standards in each case.

Planning permission

Planning permission for the main scheme must invariably be attained before work commences. Even so some clients are prepared to risk anticipating planning permission if they feel that, in the event, the planning authority will comply or condone the action because of the importance of the work.

Any good professional team knows how to build in conformity with the building regulations and/or bye-laws and all the various pieces of legislation which affect building. The team is never certain as to how the local authority will interpret every item but the variation between these points of view in real terms is likely to be a small proportion of the final cost. This risk in relation to the value of the time often makes it imperative to start as soon as possible.

Hierarchy of decisions

None of the items above will necessarily inhibit work commencing on site. The preparation of foundations, drainage, frame, brick and block walls, roofing, windows and the main lines of the services can be let. Not until the lead time for the floor screed thicknesses has to be decided, do final decisions concerning floor finishes and carpets have to be made. Window sill heights will have been determined and this will be a direct control upon the vertical key dimensions for built-in furniture. However, their design can follow at a much later stage. It can be finalized when the building is already well out of the ground. To give another example from orthodox practice; shop fitting cannot be designed until the shop tenants are identified.

Paying the builders

There is a well established system for making payments to builders. Where a QS is employed it is customary for him to visit the site once a month to value the total work done and the materials delivered, and he advises the architect accordingly. The architect then checks whether the work is satisfactory, deducts an agreed percentage, usually 5% for the retention fund, and the amounts of previous payments, and then certifies on a standard form to the client the amount due that month. The client is duty bound under the provisions of the contract to honour the certificate within 14 days, otherwise the builder may exercise his right to end the contract. The retention fund is built up month by month until the building is at the stage of 'practical completion'. Practical completion can be defined as the stage when the client can use the building safely and without reasonable inconvenience. Then it is usual to release half of the retention to the builders. The remainder is then held until the builders have completed everything, including rectifying any defects, when the architect's final certificate releases the remainder. Under the ACA Contract the retention is not released until the final certificate, thus encouraging the contractor to rectify defects promptly.

The final certificate has in the past had the legal effect of transferring to the architect some of the responsibility for the complete and satisfactory nature of the building. At least the new ACA Contract and JCT 80 iron out this twist and ensure that the builders continue to be responsible for what they have built, as in common law. Similarly, it is now realized in new forms of contract that the issuing of interim certificates does not necessarily signify that the architect is completely satisfied with the work and materials thus far fixed and supplied. Problems have a habit of manifesting themselves later.

Take-over

After practical completion the building will be inspected in detail and 'snagging lists' made of all the incomplete or unsatisfactory work. The builder has the right to make good these defects during the 'defects liability' period, usually of six months. Heating or air conditioning systems have to run for one winter and summer season to qualify for final payment.

If after the end of the defects liability period, some work still remains to be done, the client may have the work done by others, and deduct the cost from any money still owing to the builders. It is wise to get at least two quotes for such work so as to avoid the claim that the cost is unreasonably high. In any event, common law places the final responsibility on the builder to produce directly or indirectly, the agreed quantity and quality of work, in the agreed time for the agreed sum of money.

Sectional completion and directly employed contractors

A large or elaborate building may be programmed to be completed in parts, e.g. office block, labs, workshops, canteen; each being occupied by the client at practical completion. The client also has the right, if agreed at contract stage, then to bring in his own specialists, say, computer installers, laboratory equipment suppliers, catering equipment people, to complete the work and 'run-up' the operation.

Tendering

Clients and architects often find themselves under pressure from builders to negotiate direct rather than to go through the formal process of obtaining tenders from competing firms. Under certain circumstances negotiation can be a reasonable way of proceeding. These can be defined as situations where:

1 The work under consideration is part of a continuing programme of works and the rates for that work have been well established and have been externally compared as competitive.
2 The work is a repeat order where the prices have been up-dated for inflation and any incidental factors, but previous performance on other sites by the same contractor has been established as being of reasonably good value.

In all other circumstances, it is wise to go to tender. There are several important conditions which should never be overlooked:

- The bases upon which the tendering contractors bid should all be identical. In other words, the drawings should be as complete as possible, the specification and the bills of quantities should be as thorough as possible so that all the bids are on exactly the same basis. If there is room for a variation of interpretation, then the prices will vary and the bids will not be properly comparable.
- Only reputable and reliable builders should be invited to tender. It is never worth inviting firms to tender whom you have not taken the trouble to research thoroughly, and about whom you are not completely satisfied that they have a good reputation which it is in their best interest to maintain.

Long tender lists are a waste of time. Not only does the client put an unnecessary number of firms to the expense and trouble of preparing tenders, and thus adding to on-costs for clients in general, but it is soon known amongst the building fraternity that a lot of tenderers have been invited, and this in turn tends to cause the directors and their estimators to take less interest in putting in a competitive bid. As a general guide it is wise to limit the number of people tendering to between three and six. For smaller items, then three is a reasonable number to aim for. However, even with this careful process of selection and limitation, one is continually surprised at the wide variation in prices from good firms for exactly comparable work.

Variability is discussed below.

Types of tender

Apart from tenders where enquiries are based upon full drawings, details, specifications, and perhaps bills of quantities, there are occasions when tenders are sought, because of a shortage of time, on the basis of schedules of rates. In this situation, the architect or quantity surveyor will prepare, perhaps in consultation with two or three tenderers, a list of items which covers most of the sort of work that is being considered.

It is helpful if such a schedule of rates can also indicate the major quantities of work involved, without going to great lengths. For instance, the number of square metres of brickwork, the numbers of standard windows and doors, the linear run of standard partitioning, the number of square metres of flooring, ceiling and so on. In this way, estimators can give approximate prices and particular rates for the materials and labour. Once the successful tenderer has been selected by these means, then the job, if it goes forward in a hurry, can be subject to final measurement by the quantity surveyor who will then go through the job in detail, measuring out the labour and materials, and then coming to a final figure. In such circumstances the quantity surveyor or architect's initial budget figures have to depend upon their skill and experience to a much greater extent than in the orthodox situation.

Negotiation

When time is of the essence and direct professional control rapid programmes are being used, it is useful for the architect or the quantity surveyor in the team to bring the leading trade contractors to table to answer questions, explain conditions and details, examine labour loading and negotiate a price structure. In some sections of the building process there will be three or more good trade contractors from whom to invite tenders. To save time it is often appropriate to hold these meetings with the winners. But from time to time, the variables inherent in the bids make it necessary, in the client's interest, to talk to two or more likely contenders.

In other sections of the building process there will be only one reputable contractor who can undertake the work to the standard and in the time required. Under such circumstances it is legitimate for the architect or quantity surveyor to negotiate the details of their bid and the labour loadings proposed. It is of course, important that these negotiations are open and above-board and it must be made clear to the client that he is free to attend such negotiations if he so wishes.

Variability

Tenders can vary because of a number of interlocking factors:

- Fullness or otherwise of the contractor's order book.
- Desire by the contractor to gain a foothold with a particular client, or in a particular class of work.
- The contractor's perception of the profitability of a particular type of work.
- A contractor's desire to keep 'in' with a particular professional team.
- A contractor may already have work in the locality of the proposed job and would therefore save overheads if the contract's manager of the local job can oversee the new work.
- To provide continuity to an established team.

It is a very unusual building type for which typical costings are either rare or unknown. The architect or quantity surveyor in his role as building economist, will, if he is competent, be able to assess, reasonably closely all the variable factors.

4

The architect's involvement

Trends and efficiency

The architect's role in times past was essential to the construction process. For it was he who selected and controlled the master mason, master carpenter, master carver, master plasterer, and so on. He visited the site frequently and was on close terms with the trade contractors constructing the building. The rump of this process can still be seen in the Scottish separates trade contract methods but, more remarkably, it is common practice in Germany where it is flourishing strongly. It is now a growing part of North American practice, about 30% of total. But in this country, the role of the main contractor has changed, within the last two decades, to that of middle-man in the process. It is sad to note that in the relative positions of the efficiencies of the building industries, English practice is apparently the least efficient by all the standard methods of comparison. This is not to say that the main contractors themselves are inefficient, but it appears that factors such as the long lines of communication with its many breaks, together with the lack of personal responsibility and the diffused methods of control, are the underlying reasons.

Pros and cons of site meetings

As a result of the increase in the relative strength of the main contractor under the latest form of JCT Contract, the client's role, and with that the architect's role and influence, has been diminished. The contractor now has the right to run the contract as he sees fit and to claim extra payments and extensions of time over a wide range of items. Significantly, he has complete control over all the sub-contractors and it has now become the custom, and this is a relatively recent innovation, to hold the 'real' site meetings with the sub-contractors (trade contractors) independently of the meetings on site with the architects, engineers, quantity surveyor and the building owner. More and more these meetings with the design team and building owners become window-dressing affairs without any real bite. It becomes very frustrating and time wasting for the participants. As a result a school of thought has grown up which suggests that site meetings for client, architect and builder are a waste of time and should be dispensed with. Indeed, when main contractors play this particular game, one is bound to feel in some agreement with this view. This is not to say that there are not main contractors who do their best to help the client and his architect to become properly involved with the contract and to contribute to the success of the final scheme. Thus one can say that where the architect has direct involvement with trade contractors, then site meetings are valuable, or, alternatively, where the main contractor sincerely finds the contribution that the design team can make during the contract process as valuable, then site meetings are justified. If the game is played strictly by the rules of the latest form of JCT Contract, then it would be possible, as some architects now claim, for the contracts to run without the formality of site meetings. In this situation the architects would visit the site from time to time as 'policemen' to see if the quality of material and workmanship are to the standard specified.

Trends are now developing for the writing of contracts such as the ACA 2nd Edition, which give back some of the responsibility for management to the architect, and because of this, the device of the site meeting becomes, once again, of critical importance.

Minutes

In terms of the law, properly authenticated minutes (corrected and signed 'as a correct record') are invaluable for they are a fair record of the meeting, *agreed* by those present, whereas letters and other unilateral documents can be disputed. Where arbitration or litigation are involved lawyers almost always have difficulty in achieving the complete disclosure of all the documents. On top of that, not all the people concerned on the job are available as witnesses in the case, and memories are imperfect. Authenticated site minutes of complete site meetings are the best record.

Three approaches

There are three broad categories of contract, each of which make different levels of demand on site meetings:

1 Orthodox (JCT, ACA, GC works 1).
2 Management Contracts (e.g. Bovis).
3 Direct professional control (AMM).

New forms of contract (ACA), in turn, have three levels of architect involvement at the construction phase:

1 The conventional form where the architect produces a set of contract drawings which are augmented during the construction period with drawings and details that may become necessary from time to time.
2 The form where the architect, at tender stage, publishes a list of drawings that he will prepare during the course of the contract, together with a programme giving the dates upon which each drawing will be issued. The contractor then incorporates this information in his own construction programme, allowing for the adjustment of times to suit the drawing issue programme.
3 The form where the architect, at tender stage, produces a finite

set of drawings and details which describe the job in sufficient detail for the contractor to build the building in accordance with the aims and intentions so published. Thereafter, if the contractor requires any further drawings or details, he must have them prepared at his own expense. For this, he can either employ his own architects or he can commission the principal architect to do the work for a fee. In Georgian times, relatively few drawings were produced for each of the great buildings of the time, – a dozen or so, and there was sufficient information in them for the contractor to interpret the rest of the building in accordance with their spirit and intentions.

Separation of the design and construct concepts

For some reason, which is not immediately apparent, it has become customary in the building industry, to think of the design and construction processes as entirely separate. This has been reflected in the conditions of the JCT Contract, which has artificially separated out and isolated each process. It is based upon the concept that the design and drawing work can be done academically distanced both in time and space from the construction work. This is a serious error as can be illustrated in many ways. Take for example the work of a joiner erecting built-in furniture. During this process, however good the set of drawings and details, he will make many design decisions. At the larger scale, the trade contractor, in interpreting the spirit and intention of the basic set of drawings, is bound to make many natural design assumptions from the typical drawings and details. It would be wholly uneconomic and impractical for every part of the building to be completely drawn and detailed, except for work like shop fitting.

It is therefore important that in modern forms of contract, the continuing influence of the design process should be recognized as working through, during the construction process.

Site control and parallel work

In traditional contracting there are many places where there is third or second hand communication between the trade contractors and the design team. The site agent becomes in effect the communicator in spite of the fact that he was not privy to the myriad design decisions that were taken during the first five stages. (Figure 4.1).

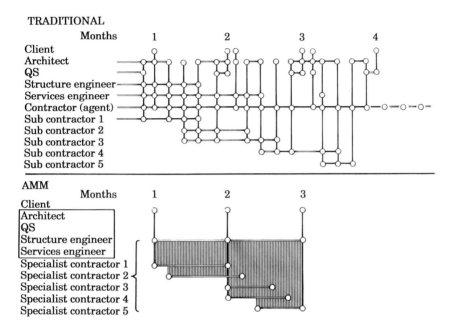

Figure 4.1 *In traditional contracts the design team communicates with the site contractors indirectly, through the site agent, whereas in AMM the communication is direct.*

In contrast, in the AMM approach, where the design team are fully involved on site, there is coherent first hand communication with the trade contractors.

Programming

There are several types of programme used in site management (Figures 4.2 and 4.3), e.g. bar chart, labour loading, CPN (Critical path net) diagrams by computer, and CPN nets to time (manual).

Architects and engineers are familiar with preparing programmes for the drawing office work and also overall programmes for the complete operation for the client's benefit. Main contractors also have the responsibility to prepare programmes. These are often a requirement in the contract documents. The programme is a working tool which needs bringing up to date regularly. Its principal object is to keep all those involved informed as to the relative state of play at any particular time so that the whole operation undertaken by a large number of people can be co-ordinated intelligently.

Bar charts, (Figure 4.2), though they are considered a little 'old hat' are nevertheless a very useful and practical working tool as they are understood by all the members of the building team. They are still of practical use on site as a clear method of communication. However, they have the disadvantage that they do not immediately indicate the critical paths through the programme. In other words, where the work of one trade happens to be a key to the timing of other operations the inter-relationship of the activities is not immediately shown by a bar chart.

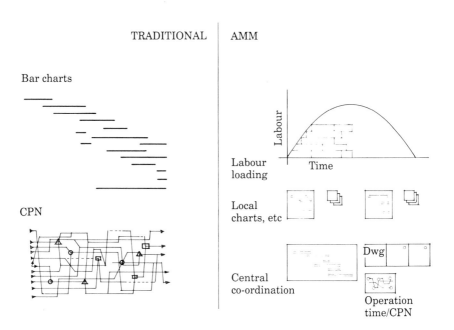

Figure 4.2 *Bar charts are traditional and readily understood, critical path nets (CPN) may be confusing for the uninitiated. Labour loading graphs are a useful tool. A design site office can provide comprehensive information in a variety of ways.*

A critical path network does show these interactions, by linking up the beginnings and ends of horizontal lines of activity to those other activities upon which it is dependent, (Figure 4.2). Critical path nets by computer can become very complicated and only really comprehended by the programmer himself. The object of the programme is to communicate to those people most concerned, and if these are the operatives on site then the programme must be readily intelligible by them. It is therefore important that for such networks the number of activities shown by the network should be reduced to not more than 30. This may necessitate some crudeness of scale but it is important that complexity is eschewed. CPN nets can be done to micro, medium and macro scale. The appropriate scale must be selected from the point of view of the recipient rather than from the point of view of the cleverness of the author.

Another point to make is that engineering design, and this includes programme design, should not be initiated by computer. It is, however, satisfactory to check a manual programme by computer. There are, at the time of writing, two important buildings in London whose structure was designed by computer rather than by engineers. In one case the reinforcement is the wrong way round and in the other case the reinforcement was 10% of what it should have been. In both cases the writs in the high court were for tens of millions of pounds. Similarly serious errors can occur with computer programming, therefore it is essential that the initial programme is set up by a competent person manually, and then, if necessary, checked by computer. Routine adjustments to the manual programme can then be tested by computer if necessary. This is a useful facility.

The great thing about the manual critical path nets is that they can be drawn on the basis of a horizontal time scale (Figure 4.3) whereas a true CPN is not drawn to a time scale. Small scale programmes can be drawn, and amended, on the conference room table in just a few minutes so that all those present can see how an adjustment to one or more of the operations can affect the progress of the work. With a large job it may be necessary to draw small CPN's for the individual information stations in various parts of the site, so that local teams can see how their work relates to others.

The labour loading graph is a useful technique for planning

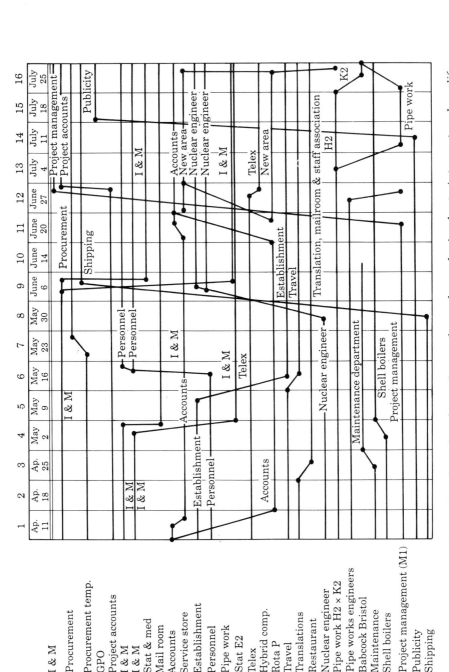

Figure 4.3 Critical path nets hand produced to a time scale can be made simpler to interpret and modify, and can focus on essential operations.

the disposition of labour forces during the progress of the works. Each characteristic horizontal line indicates the length of time for which a particular trade will be required. The vertical dimension shows the number of people employed. The important thing is to ensure that the decay rate is not too steep, otherwise it will indicate frenetic activity on site towards the end of the job. The labour loading graph also indicates the maximum forces at the height of the job. In most cases this should be kept to below 120. Above this number there can be problems of labour management and disputes. In this context it is worth noting that reliable trade contractors will not take on unknown staff even though they have a programme hot spot. An over-eager firm that takes on too many strangers and is not able to shed them if their work is unsatisfactory within the legal time limit for such action, runs the risk of strikes and other labour problems.

From Figure 2.1 it can be seen that for a conventional operation there is a critical break in communication which occurs at the end of the production drawing and tendering stage, at which point the architect has co-ordinated all the information. Once the main contractor has been selected, the whole package is handed over to the site agent who then has to learn the whole process from scratch, build the building and massage his claims files. This is a terrible disadvantage from the client's point of view, yet it is accepted with equanimity by the industry as being somehow the natural course of events. Where the professional team deals directly with the trade contractors, as with AMM/DPC, then such a break does not occur, and this is more efficient as an organizational method. It all basically depends upon the quality and experience of the people and their ability to collaborate with one another. A good organization operated by mediocre people will still produce mediocre results, whereas it is always possible for good people to operate a mediocre organization, so long as the authority operating the mediocre organization is half asleep. Once good people in a poor organization are forced to stick to the rules and are disciplined for breaking the rules, then even good people are unable to make a poor system work. The design and construction of a building is a serious and costly business and should be given the very best environment in which to operate. Hence the essential need for continuity right through the design, production drawing, tendering and site execution process. With AMM/DPC it will be seen that the team does see the job right through from start to finish.

Labour information at bills of quantities stage

In his measurement of the drawings for the bills of quantities it is quite possible for a good quantity surveyor to take off the 'time' for each of the groups of operations (Examples 4.1, 4.2 and 4.3). This data is available in most of the standard builders' price books and it is reasonably reliable although it needs interpreting with some experience of the practical problems within the building process. But it is quite within the competence of the surveyor. There is no need for him to give times for each individual item, groups of items may be timed, e.g. door sets including frames complete 'as fixed', rather than the individual items. This is known as a Specification and Estimate of Cost and Time (SECT) (see Figure 4).

EXAMPLE 4.1

Activity
Ground Slab Construction
Item   Hardcore 250, blinding, 1200 gauge polythene dpm, 150 thick concrete slab-reinforced with one layer of A 252 fabric reinforcement.

	Quantity	Rate £	Total Cost £	Material Content £	Labour Hours	Labour Days	Programme Time Days
Phase 1	2,167 m²	15.27	33,090.09	24,877.16	1,014	127	16 (8)
Phase 2	755 m²	15.27	11,528.85	8,667.40	353	44	5.5 (8)

Unit cost/m²	Labour	Material	Total
Level and consolidate	0.46	—	0.46
Hardcore	0.20	3.90	4.10
Dpm	0.33	0.28	0.61
Concrete	2.00	5.85	7.85
Fabric	0.80	1.45	2.25
	3.79	11.48	15.27
	24.8%	75.2%	100%

@ £8.10 per hour = 0.468 hours

EXAMPLE 4.2

Activity
Suspended Ceiling
Item   'Slim Wire' ceiling exposed suspension grid off of existing structure.

	Quantity	Rate £	Total Cost £	Material Content £	Labour Hours	Labour Days	Programme Time Days
Phase 1	400 m²	17.02	6,808.00	5,188.00	100.0 pair	12.5	6.25
Phase 2	390 m²	17.02	6,637.80	5,058.30	97.5 pair	12.2	6.10
Phase 3	372 m²	17.02	6,331.44	4,824.84	93.0 pair	11.6	5.80
	1,162 m²		19,777.24	15,071.14	290.5 pair	36.3 pair	18.15

Unit cost/labour analysis	Materials – bars and tiles	12.97
	Labour – 0.25 hour/pair	4.05
		17.02

Type of Building   –   Office Industrial
Work Category   –
Item Code   –

EXAMPLE 4.3

Activity
Internal Door Set
Item   Timber lining, stops, architrave, ½ hour ply faced door type 1; ironmongery

	Quantity	Rate £	Total Cost £	Material Content £	Labour Hours	Labour Days	Programme Time Days
	52	120.05	6,242.60	1,705.08	210.60	26.3	6.6 (4)

		Labour	Material	Total
Unit Cost/no.	Lining and stop	6.52	21.45	27.97
	Architrave	4.25	6.70	10.95
	Door	13.12	34.11	47.23
	Ironmongery	8.90	25.00	33.90
		32.79	87.26	120.05

@ £8.10 per hour = 4.05 hours

Woodwork	Quantity & Rate		Man Days	£
Ground Floor				
Provide and fix door and frame to vault, reusing external door to existing rear area.	1 No.	100	0.5	100.00
Provide and fix new external door with glazed panels in existing frame made good.	2 No.	150	1	300.00
Make good and leave in good working order 2 No. sash windows.	20 No.	75	15.5	1,500.00
Existing cupboard to be used for electrical switch gear to be lined with 'superlux' or similar including door, 9 mm thick.	11 m^2	12	0.5	132.00
Supply cupboard and shelving unit.	Provisional	Sum	6	500.00
Provide and fix 1,981 × 762 × 44 ply faced door and softwood frame type 1.	20	120.05	10	2,401.00
Provide and fix new pair of hatch doors each leaf 500 wide × 1,000 high and softwood frame.	1 No.		1	100.00
Provide and fix new pair of doors each leaf 610 × 1,980 × 35 in frames with 18 rebate and door closers.	2 No.	300	2	600.00
Provide and fix 150 × 25 softwood skirting.	100	3.40	1.3	340.00
			37.8	5,973.00

By courtesy of Cost Consultants, Wrightson, Pitt & Emett

This timing information can then be used by the professional team to draw up its first labour loading chart and its main CPN. When the individual tenders arrive from trade contractors, it is possible to reconcile the trade contractor's own idea of the time for the operations, with that provided by the surveyor. If there are discrepancies, then this indicates the need for further consultation to identify problems. This is one benefit.

The main benefit is that any operation which is taking unnecessarily long, can be dealt with by the allocation of additional resources of men and materials. Another trade contractor of a similar sort working in parallel in another part of the site may be the solution. In this way a positive programme can 'fast track' without danger and with positive benefit to the progress of the works and to the morale of all those taking part.

Overlay drafting and CAD (Computer Aided Design)

At the time of writing computer aided design has been over-sold to the building professions, particularly to architects. Hardware costs of between £60,000 to £100,000 are not uncommon, with software, maintenance and staffing costs of a similar order. For the average practice capital costs of this size are crippling. Their workload may not correspond with the steady throughput of large-scale work of a repetitive nature that is necessary to make CAD economical. Seven hospitals in sequence for a good paying client is the sort of workload for which computer aided drafting would be an economic approach. Large programmes of standard housing may justify a low cost CAD installation. In a practice where there is a wide variety of work and discontinuity of job input, then the taking on a relatively large capital burden is not a good recipe for survival. This is certainly true for small and medium size architectural firms. The situation is changing; genuinely user-friendly CAD software is coming more widely available (1993) as will cheap hardware with sufficient memory.

The main problem, as explained by Laserscan of Cambridge, is the difficulty of manually digitizing drawings. Whereas it is comparatively straightforward with laser techniques to digitize contours which are continuous, discontinuous lines on production drawings involve an extremely laborious, time consuming and boring repetitive operation. There is equipment now available which can 'read' drawings and digitize them. There is the parallel problem of separating out the different levels of information that any one drawing contains. The average reader-digitizer is, as yet, unable to do this.

The Americans appreciated this problem long ago. They have contrived the intermediate technology solution known as 'overlay drafting' or 'pin bar' drafting (Figure 4.4). It is interesting to note that Farmer and Dark, 25 years ago evolved a system which philosophically is the same as overlay drafting. But at that time the photographic or reprographic techniques were not available. It is now possible to blow back (enlarge) from an A4 size photographic negative to an A0 or an A1 size of drawing without loss of accuracy, registration or line definition, but note that you cannot blow back from microfiche or formats

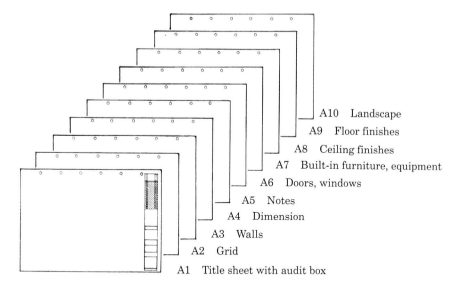

A10   Landscape
A9   Floor finishes
A8   Ceiling finishes
A7   Built-in furniture, equipment
A6   Doors, windows
A5   Notes
A4   Dimension
A3   Walls
A2   Grid
A1   Title sheet with audit box

Architect

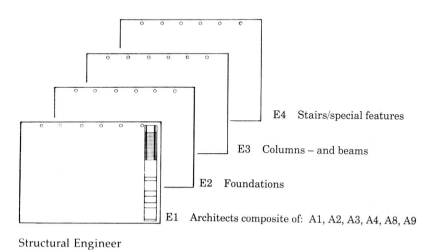

E4   Stairs/special features
E3   Columns – and beams
E2   Foundations
E1   Architects composite of: A1, A2, A3, A4, A8, A9

Structural Engineer

Figure 4.4 *The use of overlay drafting.*

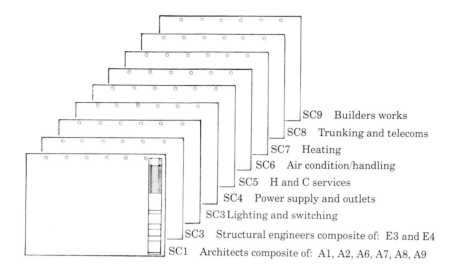

SC9   Builders works

SC8   Trunking and telecoms

SC7   Heating

SC6   Air condition/handling

SC5   H and C services

SC4   Power supply and outlets

SC3 Lighting and switching

SC3   Structural engineers composite of: E3 and E4

SC1   Architects composite of: A1, A2, A6, A7, A8, A9

Services Consultant or Contractor

smaller than photographic negatives of approximately A4. Flat bed printing machines enable composites to be made from overlays up to 4 in number. If composites of a larger number than 4 are required then 2 lots of 4 are made and from the 2 sub-composites a final composite of 8 overlays can be produced.

The great principle of overlay drafting, as in CAD, is that a separate drawing is made of each level or aspect of a job such as:

Grid
Column bases
Structure
External Walls and principal internal walls (fire compartments)
Partitions
Doors and windows
Electrics
Sanitary plumbing
Heating
Built in furniture
Floor finishes
Ceiling finishes
Special ventilation or air-conditioning
Notes

Dimensions
External services
Landscape
Roads and paths
Other external items

Not all of these items need to be kept separate in origination. The above list shows the principle. It will be appreciated that if the whole team uses the same overlay drafting discipline then there is no need for either the structural engineer or the services engineers to re-draw any of the architect's basic drawings (Figure 4.4). This is frequently done in the orthodox method. The drawings supplied to the structural engineer and the various departments of the services consultants are composites made up of the 'appropriate levels' from the list indicated above. The list above is not unique or inviolate in any way and should be carefully considered at the beginning of each new job. Each 'level' must have an extended title panel to allow for entries covering the levels to be produced by all the other disciplines. Thus, it can be seen which levels have been used to make up the composite drawing.

It will be seen that the 'notes' are a 'unique' – a separate overlay – because if the notes are done on the face of each level they likely to interrupt each other. Each discipline will require a unique notes sheet for its own particular levels.

Checking drawings is now becoming a nightmare. By using this method the whole business is simplified. By ordering composites to be made of, say, the electrics drawings with heatings drawings it can be seen if there are any collisions of socket outlets and radiators, door swings and heating equipment, light fittings etc. To have to check these things on separate dyelines is a much more difficult task. Architects are being held legally responsible for errors in co-ordinating the work of other disciplines. This is in spite of the acceptance of co-ordinating responsibility by main services contractors.

The adoption of the techniques of overlay drafting also makes the business of co-ordinating site services, structure, partitions etc. much simpler for the construction manager on site.

A word of warning: it is necessary to persuade and advocate the use of overlay drafting techniques to colleagues in other disciplines and to get their collaboration if the benefit of the method is to be enjoyed. Needless to say the Americans have been enjoying the benefits of the technique for many years. We in the UK have been slow to take advantage of this elementary and elegant method.

For the overlays polyester sheet is used, 0.04 mm thickness with one side matt. Holes are punched by the supplier either along the top edge or along one side of the sheets to fit pin bars which are made of stainless steel with brass studs accurately centred to match the holes. The sheets are taped with drafting tape to the drawing board. This is all that is required to ensure perfect registration of one drawing to the next. Fast drying inks are used in pens, which should be of the tungsten carbide tipped variety which do not wear out on the tougher polyester surface. There are limitations as to line thickness if the photographic blow back method is used. Special erasers are used for the ink which make drawing in ink very easy. It is like pencil work in that the moistened plastic eraser removes the line immediately and without scarifying the surface. When final drawings have been prepared, permanent drawings can be made for storage, and a library can be formed of the A4 negatives. This makes document transport for overseas contracts much simpler. Reductions or enlargements can be made by photographic means in order to bring drawings of different scales to the same scale.

Other methods for drawing communications

Recently large format photocopiers that can enlarge or reduce have become available. Paste-ups can be made of useful details and copied to any scale. My office has used such a machine for a period and it is an interesting and attractive process. However, it is a considerable outlay and not one perhaps for a small or medium size office to use. Large offices can no doubt justify the cost. There is some criticism at the present time that it does not 'blow-back' sufficiently accurately for the registration required for overlay draughting as the other methods referred to. Before taking the equipment on, the accuracy of blowing back (enlarging) should be carefully checked.

The use of paste-ups applies to all the methods described here and enables the architect or engineer to use details from previous jobs which apply to a particular case. There is no need to re-draw the wheel every time, let alone re-invent it.

Photogrammetry is another technique that can be an economic proposition. This uses high resolution cameras to reproduce photographed elevations accurately in drawn form. The process saves the architect or surveyor many hours measuring and plotting. It is a technique not dissimilar to that used for the accurate aerial survey of sites.

All the techniques mentioned help the site management process by producing information which is designed to be comprehended in the simplest and most direct way by those for whom it is intended. It is no good producing clever coded technical drawings for the carpenter who has the job of setting out the roof carcassing, or the joiner setting out built-in furniture. He has no technical reference documents at his elbow. He must be able to read from the face of the drawing precisely what is wanted and to what standard. Codes may take less room on the drawing and show off the skill and technical knowledge of the draughtsmen, but they are pretty useless to the operative. This is not to say that codes cannot be used in the specification where they may be read by experts in the buyers' departments of larger contractors' offices. Where the specifications or bill of quantities description is aimed at the office of a small but expert trade contractor, straightforward terms should be used which describe understood techniques and recognizable materials.

5

Financial considerations

The role of the quantity surveyor

Except for smaller schemes, or schemes where the architect is familiar with the quantity surveying process and is prepared to undertake this work for the client, it is usual to have a quantity surveyor as part of the team. He may be a partner in the firm or part of an in-house organization. Alternatively he may be a partner or senior person from an independent firm of quantity surveyors. As has been mentioned the origin of the quantity surveyor's job was in the preparation of measurement documents to provide a basis of comparison for all the builders' tenders. Over the years this work of measurement crystallized into the 'standard method of measurement', which is now in its seventh edition. It has been said that the bills of quantities represent 90% of the work in 10% of the descriptions and 10% of the work in 90% of the descriptions. In other words the measurement of all the labours in minute detail took a disproportionate amount of the work of the description. The small detail can be conveniently covered by a percentage and this means that, apart from exceptional circumstances, the bills may reduced in bulk. Another problem has emerged in that many of the standard methods of describing work do not readily fall into line with the description commonly used by the estimators in the contractors and suppliers offices.

As example, in the London area the decorating trade contractors often describe, for their own use, the quality of jobs as being one of four standards:

Boardroom
Offices
Private housing
Council housing

If 'boardroom' standard is required by the architect but the trade contractor has only priced for the supervision and workmanship to an 'offices' standard, then the architect is going to be dissatisfied with the quality of the work produced. Arguments are bound to ensue. The work may have to be condemned. The cost of rectification will be an extra burden. The programme may be disrupted. There will be claim and counter claim. If, however, the standard that is actually required is made clear to the estimator so that he can price accordingly, then the chances of argument are much less likely.

It is interesting to compare the way in which the American trade contractors measure and tender for work with that of their UK counterparts. The American process is very slick and abbreviated. The prices received are highly competitive. It has been said that the existence of the quantity surveyor in the UK doubles the number of drawings that are required from the architect because he is accustomed to calling for additional drawn information at billing stage.

The upshot of this situation is that QS's role is changing to the more important role of 'building economist'. On larger schemes his help in producing cost plans and cash flow forecasts by computer is invaluable, especially in relation to evaluations that are made of the market value of completed space projected at stages A and B.

The role of the quantity surveyor is increased when the scheme is done by AMM and he becomes an integral member of the professional team. It would be difficult to conceive of any substantial new-build job being undertaken without his skilled involvement. However, this does require a radical rethink of the QS role. It requires a preparedness to work closely with the architect and structural engineer for a much more open vision of the whole business of giving a really good service to the client.

Choice of contract

The quantity surveyor, where he is part of the professional team, from time to time takes under his wing the administrative work surrounding the choice, modification and use of the contract. In selecting the type of contract to be used the coverage of the following characteristics should be examined.

1 *Contractors' skill and care*
   The contractor shall exercise all the skill care and diligence to be expected of a properly qualified and competent contractor experienced in carrying out work of a similar scope, nature and size.
2 *Priority of documents*
   It is useful to have a provision allowing for the odd occasion when other contract documents may need to prevail over the form of agreement. A space should be allowed in the document for the insertion of the title of the document concerned.
3 *Drawings and details*
   It is useful to have the opportunity in the form of agreement to allow for the alternative to the orthodox process wherein the architect supplies a finite set of drawings. It is then the business of the contractor to provide and submit for approval such additional drawings and details that he may require during the course of the work. Needless to say, it is necessary for the contractor to understand fully the position before he signs the contract. It is also necessary for him to know what drawings and details comprise the finite set.

   This follows the North American practice and saves a great deal of unnecessary drawing and detailing that may otherwise be called for.
4 *Time schedule*
   It is useful to have as part of the contract a form which sets out:

   - The dates of the possession of the site.
   - The trades and stages which are of contractual importance.
   - When the taking over of the works by the employer and the commencement of the maintenance period should be.

- The rates of liquidated and ascertained damages.
- The expiry of the maintenance period.

A variation of this time schedule is necessary where there is sectional practical completion.

Part of the time schedule should set out a list, with dates, of the drawings, details or document to be supplied by the architect to the contractor or submitted by the contractor to the architect during the course of the works.

5 *Access to workshops by the architect*
It is necessary to provide for the free access of the architect to the works and to the trade contractors' workshops.

6 *Contractor's management of the works*
The contractor must be required to provide the necessary inspection, superintendence, supervision, planning and management for the duration of the works. It is also necessary to specify that he shall appoint an agent, to whose appointment the architect needs to consent, to act as the full time representative of the contractor on site, in charge of the works. The replacement of this person must be subject to prior written consent by the architect. It is also necessary to state that people employed on the sites must be properly skilled, qualified and experienced in their respective trades.

7 *Insurance*
The conventional insurance clauses must be included.

8 *Termination by employer or contractor*
It is necessary to include the usual clauses to cover these items.

9 *Oral instructions*
It is useful to have a paragraph about the legitimacy of oral instructions as long as they are backed up by written instructions within a specific time.

10 *Sub-letting*
Modern forms of contract seek to reduce the power of the architect and his client to nominate sub-contractors. Until about 20 years ago there was no difficulty in this area. However, now it is quite usual to find the nominated sub-contractor or supplier being blamed for delays and thus used as a reason for a claim. This mechanism has caused a great deal of adversarial posturing and even litigation. But it is essential that the client is able, through his architect, to

nominate the most appropriate and skilled specialist to execute works of most importance.

It is a practical method to 'name' the required trade contractors or suppliers in the contract document. In this instance the tendering contractors will observe the names when tendering and be able to discount or load their prices accordingly. In addition, it is sensible to list the names of the trade contractors or suppliers from whom prices will be sought later on. This is so that the contractor, at the time of tendering, may object to any particular firms on the list. A third parallel solution is to allow the 'naming' of trade contractors or suppliers after the signing of the contract but with the provision that the contractor may reasonably object.

11 *Negotiations with sub-contractors*:
In order to counteract the distancing of the constructors of the job, namely the trade contractors, from the architects and engineers, it is useful to include provisions whereby the architect is invited to the contractor's negotiations with the sub-contractors and with suppliers. Provision should also be made for the detailed records and accounts with the sub-contractors and suppliers to be made available for inspection and checking.

12 *Termination of sub-contractors*
If trade contractors or suppliers do not execute the work to the required standard and/or to programme, then provisions should be made in the form of agreement for their contracts to be terminated quickly to enable other similar trade contractors to be brought on site.

13 *Duplication*
It is also important to allow the facility for the architect to require a second trade contractor or supplier to be brought in in parallel with the particular sub-contractor if he is falling behind on programme. The only proviso here is that there must be sufficient space or distance between the two firms concerned. Close rivalry can have unpleasant consequences.

14 *Design by sub-contractors or suppliers*
Where sub-contractors or suppliers do the design of any work, the main contractor should be held fully responsible for the design. If it is an AMM contract then the situation is much clearer, for the trade contractor will have a direct

contract with the employer and thus his responsibility will be direct.

15 *Contractor's responsibility for sub-contractors*

It is necessary to ensure that the contractor is made fully responsible for his sub-contractors.

16 *Damages for delay*

There are alternative forms which may be provided for the handling of this matter. In the conventional method liquidated and ascertained damages are set down in the contract document or in an appendix. These are the best estimate as to what the damages will be if there are delays to the works by the contractor. An alternative may be provided where the employer is entitled to recover from the contractor such damage, loss or expense as may be suffered by him arising out of the contractor's default.

It is unreasonable to load trade contractors and suppliers with heavy liquidated damages. If the figures put to them are too onerous, they will either charge a higher price or they will decline the tender. The whole business of damages is a negative defence of marginal value to the employer at the time they are settled, many months, sometimes years after the end of the contract. At that time the figures concerned are of academic interest to the client and only of serious interest to the lawyers, for their fees are involved. What the client really needs is a building finished on time to the right quality and to the estimated total cost. Such damages as may be stated in the documents are only of value if they help to achieve this aim. If the general effect of the damages quoted in the documents is to make the trade contractors nervous and liable to shoot off letters in all directions in order to cover their positions, much time and effort is wasted which should otherwise be applied to the positive job of building the building properly.

The whole tenor of the job should be a positive one to build the building efficiently. The administrative procedures should not siphon off vitality in useless directions. If the trade contractor or supplier is not doing his job he should either be replaced or duplicated in the ways outlined above. Damages have little effect in the positive direction.

17 *Extensions of time*

If the job is a normal one then the orthodox clauses for the extension of time may be appropriate. If however, time is of the absolute essence then most of these clauses can be deleted and only the absolute ones should be allowed, and the acts, instructions or default by the employer or the architect on his behalf.

18 *Submission of estimates by the contractor*
It is useful to provide a mechanism whereby if a variation to the works is contemplated by the architect or his client, then the contractor is required to provide an estimate of cost and time so that a decision concerning a possible variation can be made by the client. It is necessary to allow for the instruction for that particular variation to proceed even if the price is unsatisfactory and subject to a final settlement at a later stage.

19 *Fluctuations due to inflation etc.*
Fluctuations may be permitted to the contract sum in most orthodox contracts, and is an onerous and time consuming administrative chore. There are well over 50 indices to be applied to the different trades in the JCT form. Instructions concerning fluctuations in one particular well established contract number over 100 pages. The ACA solution of having a single index which averages them all out has been tested and found to be fair within minute limits.

20 *Effect of the final certificate*
It is important that any certificate including the final certificate issued by the architect shall not relieve the contractor of his common law liability for the works.

21 *Adjudicator*
Serious consideration should be given to the nomination of an adjudicator. It is interesting to note that the British Property Federation have made the appointment of an adjudicator a mandatory part of their new management system. The adjudicator is an independent professional of considerable experience who is called in to take an instant view of a situation under dispute and to determine the way in which the contract should proceed. The parties have to agree and the matter may be opened up at arbitration or litigation. The use of the adjudicator clears the air and prevents misunderstandings putrefying away and spoiling the positive and constructive attitude of building teams.

The above list is by no means a complete list of all the items that should be covered in a contract (form of agreement). They are merely the ones which should be looked at most carefully when choosing between the various forms of contract that are currently available.

Cost prediction

In traditional contracting the client and his design team will have difficulty in anticipating trade contractors' claims and extras. The details of the tenders to the main contractor from his individual domestic trade contractors are unseen by the client or the architect and his design team. Claims can be made (and usually are) below the line. It is difficult for the design team to get a realistic view of the extras that are charged. They are not privy to the detailed information. (Figure 5.1).

With AMM the visibility of the claims and extras situation is greater because the client has a direct contractual relationship with the trade contractors.

COST PREDICTION

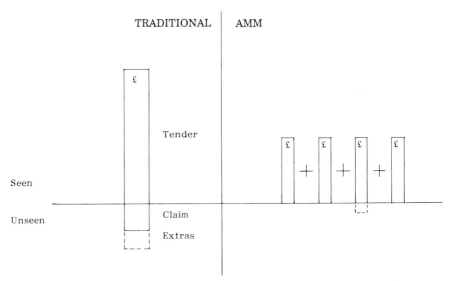

Figure 5.1 *In AMM the potential for claims and extras is more readily seen than in traditional contracts.*

6
The design team

In the past it has been quite usual for the architect to be entrusted with the task of recommending co-consultants to join the team for the design and execution of the building: namely the quantity surveyor, structural engineer, services engineer, landscape architect etc. Some institutional clients prefer to nominate the quantity surveying firm independently. The reason for this is apparently that they feel that to have a QS independent of the architect is somehow going to ensure that the QS will not be biased towards masking the architect's errors. This negative view is plausible but could only be of practical use at final account stage if the architect has been careless to the extent that he is in danger of being sued for negligence. It is rather like asking a mortician for his view of the health of the patient before he dies. A positive and more sensible approach is to ensure that the architect has a QS who he can work with and who is going to be of help and assistance in planning the scheme in the most efficient and economical way. Team work is the proper way to approach the issue rather than to set up a climate of adversarial professionalism.

The situation is more obvious with the appointment of the structural engineer.

Structural engineer

The architect must obviously have somebody with whom he can work well and closely in the structural engineering firm appointed. Theoretically the closest relationship would be that in a multi-professional practice where the structural engineer is a partner in a firm of architects. There are a few firms in the country of this type. It is a difficult situation to achieve, because most structural engineers do prefer to be independent as in this way they can gain a sufficiently wide band of experience.

Services engineers

This is a more difficult area. There are a number of firms of services engineering consultants whose conventional pro-gramme of working has been out of step with that of the architect and structural engineer. The proportion of services in building has expanded enormously in the last 30 years. There is as yet insufficient recruitment at a suitable level to the profession. The consultants have been dominated by the contracting side of the industry who still undertake a large amount of the design work. However, there is a trend developing where some professional firms are now prepared to provide a full service. The Department of Health is now insisting, in many cases, that the full service is provided. Unless this is provided, and the greater fee met, there can be a serious lack of co-ordination between the services consultant and other members of the team. A situation can develop where the services contractors and their sub-contractors can build up substantial claims.

It is highly desirable that the services consultant is brought into the team at the beginning of the job and that the client is persuaded to meet the additional fee for his full service.

For many jobs, e.g. hospital work, the amount of the services engineering work can be more than that of the architectural and structural work. It is therefore very important that the stages of work for the architect and structural engineer are the same as those for that of the work of the services consultant. The conventional process, whereby the detail design is left to the services contractor's sub-contractors at a stage many months after the main contract is let, is unacceptable and bound to produce claims and delays.

It is therefore vital that the architect is fully consulted about the appointment of the services consultant, so that he can ensure that the partners of the firm concerned are able and willing to undertake the work within the principles of the programme outlined above.

(See also *The Architect's Guide to Fee Negotiations* where the sequences and relationships are set out in detail).

Quantity surveyor

The quantity surveyor has an important contribution to make at the beginning of the scheme when various solutions are being tried and tested both structurally and economically. He must be willing to work with the architect and not against him. They both have their reputations at stake. If matters do go badly and come to court then each may have to defend his own corner. The client will not have to suffer obscuration of the facts by the collusion of these two disciplines.

The traditional form of the bills of quantity, where 90% of the work is represented by 10% of the entries and 10% of the work (i.e. the labours other small details) is represented by 90% of the entries, is now considered to be rather out of date and new methods are being promulgated. Bills of quantities were originally intended to be a basis of equality for the purposes of obtaining tenders. They can also be annotated to provide a useful working shopping list and programme material. However, now that computers are being used this facility is now more readily available and should be considered.

It is necessary for the architect to be closely involved in the selection of the firm of quantity surveyors to be employed so that he can be assured of collaboration in reaching economic and efficient construction solutions.

Landscape architect

Landscaping now becomes an important part of schemes, and is often a specific requirement of the planning authority. It is clearly of benefit to buildings to have the external environment properly clothed and furnished by trees, ground cover, etc. Some firms have landscape architects within the partnership and others appoint independent landscape architects. Whichever way is chosen, the client is well advised to allow the appointment of a skilled professional in this context rather than to rely upon the commercial garden firm, whose aims are usually different.

Continuity and manning

Ideally, the architect/engineer team, which prepares the inception and feasibility studies and goes through the scheme design, detail design and production process, should continue on site as the management team and see the job through. There are many sound reasons for this approach, some of which have been detailed elsewhere.

1 The design process involves a myriad of decisions; a buildable building requires that those decisions are understood by the executants and not altered or compromised unless increased efficiency results.
2 The team is fully aware of the reasons for all these decisions and has been through them over and over again with the client and his people, whereas a new construction manager brought on to the scene at stage K will be puzzled by some of the decisions that have been made and be out of sympathy with them and seek to change them in some way. If he had been with the scheme from the start he would comprehend the reasons for them.
3 New staff brought on at a late stage (e.g. stage K) would be starting their learning curve from the beginning and waste valuable time at a critical period.

4 It is admitted some architects and engineers prefer just to stay on the drawing board and are not particularly interested in seeing the results of their theoretical work built practically on site. However, any good designer, whether an architect or an engineer, wants to see the results of his work and his collaboration with colleagues in other professions. The excitement of the execution of a designed building is a considerable stimulus to the team and the client benefits from the release of this energy.

5 It is a great benefit to the client to be able to continue to deal with the same people with whom he has collaborated in the formulation of the original design. The establishment of this joint team and the confidence which it produces is an important asset not to be wasted.

As has already been said the building industry at the present time mistakenly conceives that there is some sort of God given division between the design process and the construction process (Figure 6.1). In reality the design process continues right the way through until the last craftsman adds his last contribution to the built form. Some trades contribute a great deal by way of design, and others relatively little, but their general importance has been ignored. The position has been exacerbated by many of the modern forms of contract separating the designer from the constructor in legal terms. From the beginning of the history of architecture and where conscious design processes have been involved, there has been a healthy feed-back between craftsmen and designer, without which the development of architecture through the ages would have been practically impossible. The extension of the knowledge of the development of materials to encompass greater spans, greater heights, development of new forms of enclosing space, the exercise of new modes of expression often with a very limited vocabulary of material, would not have happened without constant feed-back from craftsmen to designer. It is foolish to think that this valuable process can be cut off and that the understanding of the use of materials in architecture can somehow continue in a vacuum.

This legal tourniquet on the feed-back process has already caused the building industry to suffer from some morbid symptoms. There is much grumbling about the inability of the

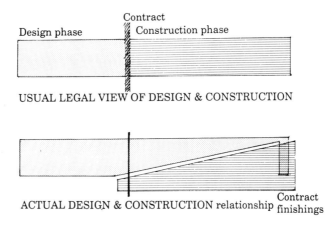

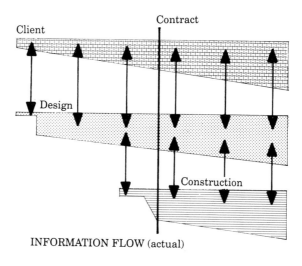

Figure 6.1 *Growth and transmission of knowledge as the job develops.*

designer to draw 'buildable' buildings and for his general lack of practical know-how. On the other side there are already many schools of architecture who eschew practical and continuous involvement with the real crafts of architecture. The academization of teaching staffs, and the rapid disappearance of the practitioner who teaches part time, is hindering the development of students able to integrate the design and construction process.

Concentration

Another inhibition to the professional person's proper con-centration on a job is that most professional people in the building industry have to cope with many jobs at different stages at any one time. Ask any mid-career architect, engineer or surveyor how many schemes he is currently dealing with and very rarely will you find that he is solely responsible for one job with no other jobs to distract him. This means that because of the wide spread of responsibility and preoccupation, the ability to predict problems and thus to be able to organize strategy to circumvent them is reduced. (Figure 6.2).

Unfortunately it is rarely possible for partners to allow themselves the luxury of looking after just one major job. However, it is possible for them to arrange for their architect members of staff to be deployed in this way if jobs are of a sufficient size to warrant it. This may not often be perfectly possible, but it is manageable in many cases for the architect to have a major portion of his time properly allocated to a single job. This is all the more possible if the job has a site office organized for it where the job architect is expected to be present for a particular part of each day.

Affordability

There is no easy rule of thumb which can be used to determine whether it is possible to afford a full time architect or engineer on site. Certainly it has been possible so to employ people for jobs of £1m or over. Other jobs of £2m have had daily visits at a specific time from local job architects or engineers. The only real way to determine this is to do a resource analysis. An example is available in *The Architect's Guide to Fee Negotiations*.

The important principle is that the trade foreman, and others on site, should be able to rely on the regular daily visit of a knowledgeable job architect/engineer so that any problems can be dealt with immediately. If operatives are held up for any period longer than 24 hours demoralization sets in and the client is in danger of having to spend money unnecessarily. If your own firm does not have offices near to the site in question then it is usually possible to find the partners or senior people of local firms of architects or engineers prepared to provide the local supervision. The important thing is that the client is properly served by on-the-spot practical information and professional action on site.

A few simple calculations will show that the faster track the job has programmed for it, then the more likely it is that daily or full

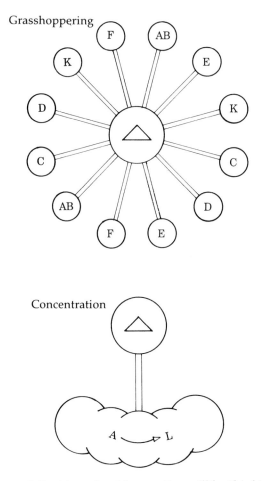

Figure 6.2 *The architect in a sizeable practice will be thinking about many simultaneous jobs, each at a different stage, ('grasshoppering'), whereas the on-site architect in AMM can concentrate on all the stages of one job, thus be more effective. (Letters represent RIBA Plan of Work stages.)*

time professional staff can be allocated to the job. If a £1m job goes through in 4 months then it can be readily seen that a 5% project management fee can cover the site professional team necessary.

In computing the cost of on-site staff remember that the start up period must be included and also a finishing off period after the job is over. For the usual fast track job two months is adequate at the beginning, and a month at the end. Do not forget to allow for the cost of office accommodation if the client cannot provide it for you, and of telephones, cleaning, part-time secretarial services, security, lighting etc. This sort of provision is much easier with rehabilitation jobs where invariably parts of the client's accommodation can be made available. However, with new construction, where conventional security fences/hoardings, site offices, site generators, etc. have to be provided, the whole thing becomes not necessarily more difficult, but certainly more elaborate. Although architects in past ages have been used to coping with these problems, in recent years this field of activity has become unfamiliar. A certain modest application of nerve and confidence is necessary when initiating this type of exercise, together with the assistance of someone experienced in evaluating site costs.

Construction manager or job architect/engineer

It is a matter of judgement whether to use a construction manager taken on the professional staff from the building industry, or whether to use an architect/engineer taken from one's own staff, or an architect/engineer taken on from a friendly neighbourhood practice for the duration of the job.

Obviously each case must be taken on its merits. A complex new built job of, say, over £2m would certainly justify the employment of a construction manager (site agent) from the building industry. It is worth taking a great deal of care to find someone who has a sufficiently 'professional' approach and who wishes to become part of the professional team. It needs to be somebody who is readily prepared to take on the job whole-heartedly on behalf of the client and able to shed the defensive claims-oriented attitudes which are so common in the industry.

A wholly positive attitude towards building is not all that difficult to find and it is amazing how enthusiastic such people become once they realize that their main task is to get on with the building in the most economical and efficient way. Scales appear to fall from the eyes when it is realized that the object of the exercise is not to exacerbate problems but to solve them.

On the other hand, a competent job architect who has demonstrated a particular interest in the buildability of buildings and in the whole process of overseeing work on site may often be an excellent candidate for the work of the construction manager because of his broader view. If he has been fortunate enough to have been closely involved with stages A to J then the continuity will be excellent. This type of manager will be good for most rehabilitation jobs, including those of some considerable complexity. The more orthodox problems of site management such as that of security, site works etc. with which some architects/engineers have less familiarity today, are not so often present with this type of work. He may need some guidance upon the suitable sequence of work. For instance it is a mistake to allow demolition of existing partitions to go on when finishing trades are operating. This type of obvious point can sometimes be missed by the enthusiastic.

When making the decision as between architect/engineer and professional construction manager from the industry, it is worth noting that, on the whole, rates of pay for the latter are higher by a factor of 20%/30%. The latter also requires a car and petrol as of right. One also needs to see some distance ahead that there will be continuity of employment. It would be unfortunate to take a professionally inclined construction manager on from the industry and then to discharge him at the end of the job. Nevertheless anyone with a reasonable degree of optimism should foresee some growth in this type of activity as part of the professional service which progressive firms of architects/ engineers can in future offer their clients.

Chairmanship and leadership

Whoever the client chooses to manage the building process will decide upon the manner in which this role is to be executed. It is obviously desirable that there are as few breaks as possible in the communication chain. Thus it is sensible for the client to take the advice of the architect or engineer on the method to be adopted. If the orthodox procedures are to be used, then the orthodox process of going out to tender to main contractors will be employed. A quantity surveyor will no doubt be appointed to prepare bills of quantity so that the tenders will all come in based upon the same basic data.

If separate trade contracts (Direct Professional Control) the AMM version is to be used, then the way the professional team operates will be under the control of the lead profession. In most types of building, as distinct from engineering work, this will usually be the architect. His job must then be to select a team of engineers, surveyors and construction managers who are not only competent and experienced but also who are also able to get on well together. It is worth emphasizing again that it is no good having incompatibilities in this key team. They will only destroy the positive and progressive attitudes that engender a determination to solve the problems in an efficient and competent manner. In this positive environment the chairman takes a relatively low profile. All he has to do is to see that the team is kept on the rails. At any one time during the team's deliberations if, say, the QS is making a valuable point concerning the relative economics of particular types of solution, then all the other members of the team will be listening to him and will take on board what he says. The surveyor will then be in effect 'leading the team'. Similarly if the engineer makes a particular point concerning the way the structure may be applied, then he at that point will be in effect 'leading the team'. In this situation it will only be necessary for the architect to ensure that the direction is maintained properly and that the meetings are not over long or allowed to wander off the point.

Minutes

Needless to say such meetings should be correctly minuted. The minutes circulated immediately after the meetings so that everyone is kept up to date as to what is going on. Even those members of the team who are not able to be present should be circulated so that their files are complete and that the 'story' is kept intact. If the client is interested in the particular stage at which the team is working and is able to provide positive input then he should be welcomed on-board.

It is worth emphasizing again that minutes must be signed as a correct record at each succeeding meeting, and incorporate any corrections that members request. Such minutes are considered by the law courts to be the most authentic record of the job. Letters or records of phone calls are unilateral and therefore, by their very nature, suspect. If only members of the industry would realize the obviousness of this point then many tons of paper could be saved each year together with aeons of wasted time. To have the privilege of being present at positive meetings such as those outlined above, is quite an inspiring experience and makes the business of working in the construction industry worthwhile. It is such a change from the usual preoccupations with claims, legal actions and complaints.

Eliminate problems at source

It is foolish to try to control mismanagement, claims etc. by elaborate site auditing or independent project management procedures during the course of the works rather than by getting the system right at the beginning.

If, for example, there is an impure water supply, it is only possible to control it by closing valve B and operating valve C (Figure 6.3). Similarly if an ineffective and over-elaborate system is set up no amount of fiddling with the equivalent of valve C will be of any real help. In other words, use competent people and firms in the first place and then trust them to get on with it. If they are not competent then no amount of 'management' later on will improve the job. On the other hand a competent firm can be snared into incompetence by checking, counter-checking and bureaucratic 'control'.

Preparation of contract drawings and documents

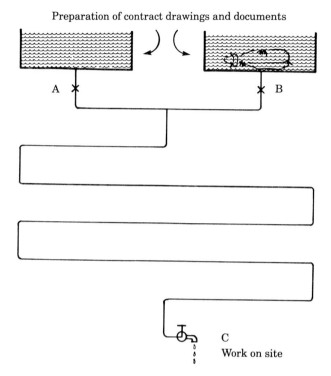

Figure 6.3 *Problems must be dealt with at source.*

7

Preliminary items and Advanced Methods of Management (AMM)

Function

Items pertaining to practical site management are known in the industry as 'prelims'. These items are listed in bills of quantities and are coped with in the orthodox way by the main contractor. In the case of a serial contract (AMM/DPC) they must be taken in hand by the construction manager whether he be the continuing job architect/engineer or a professional site agent employed by the architects or engineers.

Security

In the case of new works the site will need security defences such as a chain link or wire grid fence or a plywood hoarding. There are two schools of thought as to which one to choose; the chain link or wire grid fence, often with barbed-wire tops, allows the police and those working in the neighbourhood to see what is happening on the site. If the site is kept lit through the night then security is better. The blank hoarding prevents greedy eyes being tempted by the materials or equipment, but once the villain has gained access no one can see what he is up to. I have used both methods and find the former more satisfactory. Fencing is of course the remit of the fencing contractor and competitive quotes can be obtained.

Access

It is usual to provide only one access on the site so that it can be supervised properly from the site offices. The local authority may need to be consulted concerning the best point of access and a temporary pavement crossover authorized. Heavy lorries delivering goods to the site can damage minor roads and consideration has to be given to ensuring adequate turning circles into the site.

Advertisement revenue

Boundary fences which face traffic or populated routes may be suitable for advertisement hoardings and the client can gain some revenue. There are major hoarding contractors who will quote for the provision of hoardings and the income they are prepared to pay for the facility during the course of the works. The local authority may need to be approached for a licence for this purpose.

Site offices

Depending on the size of the job, site offices may be essential. It may be possible to provide site offices immediately adjacent to the site or, if the contract concerns an addition to an existing building, then offices may be available therein. However, for new works the mobile type of site office is likely to be required. Quotes can be obtained from a number of specialists in this field.

They will provide fully fitted offices to specification including lighting, heating and socket outlets. If temporary electrical supplies are not immediately available, then it may be necessary to hire a generator of suitable capacity to light the site and to light the offices. Heating, by propane or similar fuel, may be required.

Offices will be required for the construction manager, the site foreman (on larger jobs where the checking control and tidiness of the site need a separate direction), the job architects and engineers, and to house toilets, etc. Offices are usually provided by the trade (works) contractors for their own people and a site should be reserved for them near to the main site offices. It is also important to have a conference room for the many meetings that are involved as part of the site office complex.

Telephones

Telephones are an important part of the running of the job and it is necessary to make early provision for their installation in the site offices.

Material storage

Depending upon the type of job, thought must be given to the handling and storing of materials which are liable to damage by the weather. Whatever the material, a programme has to be prepared in order to organize the storage and care of materials on site. It may be necessary to build a special storage building for some types of operation. In other types of job, the completed carcass or part of it can be used for storage of goods which are susceptible to damage. It is necessary to ensure there is adequate security for valuable materials. Trade contractors may be required by the contract documents to provide their own material storage compounds and be responsible for their care and maintainance. One of the benefits of the ACA type of contract is that from the client's point of view the contractor is responsible for the materials and equipment until fixed into the works, thereafter they become the property of the employer. They must be covered by the contractor's insurance until completion. The position is different for work to an existing building where the owner may be responsible for insurance, depending upon the type of contract and the clauses selected.

Site roads

It is important that throughout the period of the contract, especially with new works, the access ways in the site are of a sufficient standard to remain firm throughout wet weather and maintained at a reasonable level, and can be kept clean. In some types of ground condition it may be necessary to metal the surface. It is usually possible to arrange for most of the site roads to follow the final roads of the designed scheme, in which case the hardcore, so long as it is properly maintained, is compacted by the site traffic. There are sometimes problems with mud oozing up between the particles of the hardcore and thus damaging its future bearing capacity. The use of special fibrous mats to prevent this happening is a worthwhile precaution. Obviously materials of a rugged nature such as bricks and blocks may be stored under tarpaulins but it is important that the bases upon which they are put are carefully organized to ensure that mud and vehicle damage does not occur and that they will not get in the way of subsequent operations.

Scaffolding

In the case of work to existing buildings it may be that only one trade requires the use of scaffolding. In this case it may be convenient to make him responsible for the inclusion of scaffolding in his contract. If scaffolding is going to be required throughout the course of the job, then this can be made a separate preliminary item. However, it is worth pointing out that on many contracts observed throughout the country scaffolding is erected in position and remains unused for long periods of time. It is an expensive additional cost and rationalization is worthwhile. Another approach is to make one trade contractor, usually the one who is going to use the scaffolding most, responsible for the scaffolding, with the proviso that he permits other trades to use it as and when this is necessary. This needs to be spelled out clearly at the enquiry stage.

Mechanical goods handling

It is often necessary to arrange special plant for the handling of materials into and out of the site, such as cranes, chutes, hoists, conveyors, etc. The quantity surveyor is able to assess the amount of movement that the projected programme requires. With this basic information the plant trade contractors should be consulted as to the most appropriate plant. They are expert and helpful and often economies can be achieved by ensuring that the right type of plant is on site for each particular stage. This is a fascinating part of the process and it is well worth taking the trouble to consult the experts concerned.

Safety

Safety is now a major matter to be dealt with on site. It is necessary to ensure that all those working on the site during the appropriate stages wear hard hats. These should be made readily available by the trade contractors for their people. A supply should be made available in the site office for visitors and the main site office staff. The provision of toe boards and handrails at all exposed positions are an essential part of the safety programme. The local authority usually has a safety officer who will visit the site and wield a legal stick if the precautions are not properly followed. A good scaffolding contractor knows the form. It is necessary to have somebody trained in first aid on site. This can be done by sending an assistant member of the team on a short course. It is a useful skill to have in any event. If accidents occur then the authorities have to be notified. If roads or pavings around the site become damaged and unsafe, it is wise always to warn the local authority.

Unauthorized movement

Another aspect of security is the unauthorized movement of people in and out of the site. With new works, where there is a single enclosing security fence, the problem of overseeing the entrance and the control of unauthorized ingress is easier. On sites which are in existing occupation some system of identification labels and/or passes becomes necessary. The object is to prevent theft of materials from site.

Canteen

On all but the smallest sites it is necessary to organize some method whereby the operatives can have tea breaks etc. on site. Any sort of refreshment taken off site means continual movement of people out of the premises. There are canteen catering firms available for this type of work. The item should be dealt with in the preliminaries. It may be possible, if there is one major trade contractor, to make catering his responsibility. In any event there should be a mess room where people can have their breaks in a properly organized way. It is not satisfactory to have operatives taking breaks at their site of work. It is embarrassing to take a client on a routine site visit and to find people sitting around taking their meal breaks. It is therefore necessary to organize the refreshment arrangements with the trade contractors at the outset as part of the conditions of the job.

Checking and material storage compound

On large sites it may be necessary to employ a checker to oversee the reception of goods and check them against delivery notes, which are then passed to the office for reconciliation with orders and invoices. On sites up to, say, £3m this work could be done by the construction manager's assistant (foreman). On large refurbishment jobs, checking may require the employment of a specialist individual and an assistant. One of the problems that may arise is the completion of particular rooms or areas and their checking, snagging and locking. The issuing of keys to finishing trades becomes quite a problem and needs the allocation of staff to oversee this. It is a problem which goes on throughout the working day and can cause a waste of time to senior people unless handled by a specific individual.

Site tidiness

An index of the quality of the management of the job is that of the general condition and organization of material on site. Site tidiness takes an input of supervision and labour. But it is important to maintain it throughout the job.

Nameboards

Most sites require nameboards for the professional firms engaged and also for the trade (works) contractors. This requires an item in the preliminaries account. Other notices are required concerning the site office location, safety, and other precautionary messages.

Financial management of prelims

There are several methods which can be employed for the payment of preliminary items where there is no main contractor. One such method is to set up an imprest account under the aegis of a separate company set up for the purpose, for instance: 'Bloggs & Bloggs Germins Hospital Site Ltd.' Bloggs & Bloggs would be the name of the professional firm responsible. The fund is set up with an amount as an originating float which is then topped up month by month by the sum expended on preliminary items during the preceding month. The amounts are validated by architect's certificate, and supported by vouchers listed by the quantity surveyor. Another method would be for the preliminary items to be met item by item by the client. This would only be suitable for a small job as it would put a considerable, but not strictly necessary, burden on the client's organization.

Appendix 1
The Design–Construction Group

The paper which follows summarizes recent thinking on the future of collaborative design and construction. Taking part in the exercise are three professional firms and two construction companies. No direct experience has yet been achieved by them all working together, though sub-groups of the five have worked together successfully over the last ten years. In spite of this thinking, adversarial methods will continue into the future, but there is room for the growth of more positive approaches such as this.

The paper repeats some of the material in the main text of this book, but the concepts are summarized and linked together in an order which is more suitable for presentation to the owner and the building team.

A new design–construction concept

Introduction

This paper outlines the means whereby new building and renovation can be achieved economically and expeditiously by a totally unified approach. It proposes a new concept under which the combined skills of the designers and constructors can be available in an integrated team under responsible leadership at the very outset of the project.

This will provide benefits to the client which are clearly not available under more traditional methods of building procurement.

How can we improve on current methods of building procurement?

The hallmark of many construction projects is perceived to be confrontation. But if the builder is required to work to a fixed sum, as he usually is, some element of strain is inevitable. The strain becomes counterproductive when what the builder is required to build for a particular fixed sum is not fully or properly designed and/or he is not adequately briefed at the time that he must make the commitment.

Misunderstanding of what the building should have comprised, or when outstanding data should have been made available, erupts into large monetary claims and results in settlement being achieved usually through exasperation rather than evaluation.

A building of any quality requires thorough and competent design authorship. In the same way good music must be scored properly with all the parts, phrasing and dynamics noted. A playwright has to set down all the details, describe characterization and give the stage directions for the play to come alive. So the architect/engineer must take the concept through to detail and show how the materials and components fit together to produce an effective whole. During such a process of design craftsmanship there can be a two-way benefit from communication with the builder.

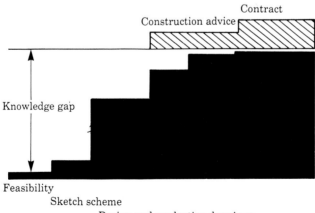

Figure A1.1 *The knowledge gap.*

In recent years, clients of the industry have experimented with new procurement methods: management contracting, design and build, construction management, to name but a few.

Many of those who espouse these new ideas do so vainly hoping that they can have their cake – a commitment to competitive price – and eat it – enjoy the luxury of not being committed to a wholly finite design sooner than they choose. The resulting almost inevitable confrontation is often primarily blamed upon the separation of the design process from the construction process.

Figure A1.2 *The usual confrontation.*

The division between design and construction is not as distinct in practice as the purists would have us believe, particularly in the field of mechanical and electrical services. Moreover, handing over the design process to the contractor does not begin to solve the inevitable problem that flows from an inadequate or incomplete brief.

No procurement system gives complete commercial certainty unless the brief for and design of the building is complete before construction is commenced. However in the case of larger more typical projects the brief evolves as the design progresses. All too often this results in the need for a continuing dialogue between the client and members of the design team, the absence of any detailed services input and insulation from the advice of the constructor.

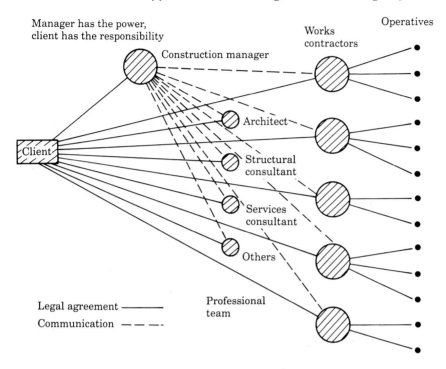

Figure A1.3 *Communication and responsibilities in construction management.*

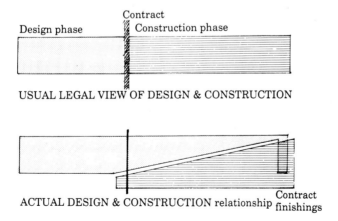

Figure A1.4 *The division between design and construction phases.*

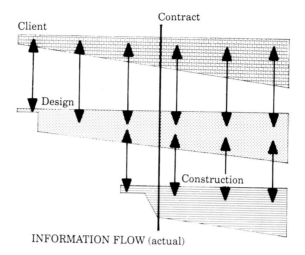

Figure A1.5 *Information flow in practice.*

The new design–construction concept

The new concept centres around a grouping together of organizations offering the following disciplines:

- Architecture and planning
- Structural and services consultancy
- Building construction
- Services engineering and construction
- Cost consultancy

Those organizations that choose to come together for the project concerned will have worked together before and will have senior partners/directors who have similar aims and attitudes, and mutual respect for one another. Their identity will depend upon the circumstances, including, of course, the client's wishes, but above all their senior partners/directors will believe in the concept and will select the personnel who are temperamentally suited to work together within a project team and can collectively offer integrated design and construction using the principles of 'simultaneous engineering'.

Simultaneous engineering is an approach where the designers and the production engineers work alongside each other. The design team no longer chases its tail seeking perfection: the production people understand more readily the design thinking and contribute to it, and the product gets to the market more quickly, in better shape. Value engineering is in place from the earliest stages so as to ensure that quality, time and cost-in-use meet the client's criteria.

The organizations will form a company to execute the project concerned. This company will be in contract with the client and will be represented by a project director. This gives the client the important advantages of a single point of contact and of not having to take any responsibility for the interfaces between each of the designers and constructors.

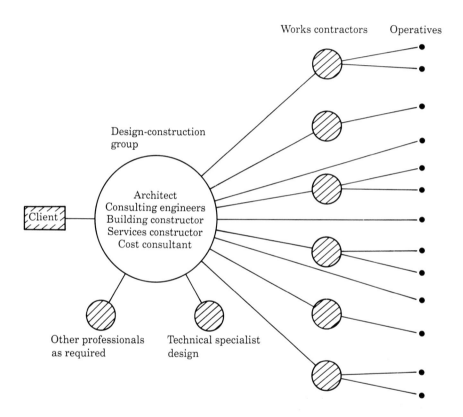

Figure A1.6 *The design-construction group contract system.*

A cornerstone of this new concept is that all the members of the company, whether of professional or contracting origins, will participate in the financial success of the venture, in such a way as to encourage open and co-ordinated working towards the successful outcome. This will turn their attention away from partisan interests and focus them upon what is in the best interest of the project as a whole.

It will be the responsibility of the company to manage its constituent members. Internally there will be a board of management and the members will work together on the round table principle. In the design phases the lead will be taken by the architect or the engineer; in the construction phase the leadership will pass to the building constructor while the building works are critical, and will then transfer to the services engineer/constructor in the latter stages when the building services becomes the critical element.

Figure A1.7 *Round table teamwork.*

As will be apparent, the members will all be highly motivated to complete the project to quality, cost and time. The constructors will carry out the work with their own workforces or through competitive subcontracts depending upon which is judged by the company to be best in the circumstances. This is just one of the many decisions which will be taken on an informed value-for-money basis by the Board which embodies all the relevant design and construction experience, including importantly those of the cost consultant.

The client or his representative will be encouraged to meet regularly with the Board to review progress, quality and cost. The further step of inviting the client to share in the profits brought about by effective joint decision-making suggests itself, and there will be the opportunity for the Agreement to provide for this. One can go still further: the client could take an appropriate equity share in the company, thereby obviating the need for a contract between the client and the design-construction company.

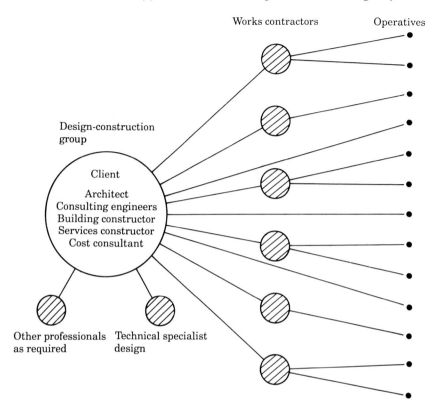

Figure A1.8 *The design-construction group contract system with client participation.*

Building owners have currently little recourse if things go wrong in a contract other than to claim negligence against their consultants and contractors in the courts. Under this new concept the client need only look to the company and to the guarantees supporting that company; how the liabilities are shared within the company will not be a concern to him. So far as insurable risks are concerned, the company will adopt European practice, whereby building insurance is taken out over ten years or longer in favour of the building owner. The cost of the insurance, termed latent defects insurance, will be an integral part of the Agreement. This will also be linked to the operation and maintenance manual requirements for the future care of the building.

Benefits

This new concept has been developed as a response to seemingly intransigent difficulties in the building industry. Sceptics will call it a compromise; practitioners will see it as an innovative but none the less realistic approach.

The client will secure an obvious benefit from employing a team of people backed by organizations that have a recognized successful track record of working effectively together. The emphasis will be on the team or joint approach to solving problems, developing the design and undertaking the construction.

This concept brings about a grouping together of the key members of the building process. It provides the prospective building owner with the possibility of a single entity capable of taking a building from commission to completion.

Major benefits to the client will be the significant reduction of time, and thus of cost, of the period from concept to the completion of his building, and the opportunity to achieve cost certainty at an earlier date.

The client will have the benefit of having procured his building without the expense and distraction of claims which are not of his own making. Lawyers benefit from strife, clients rarely do.

The involvement of the full building team from the outset provides the client with greater ease and expertise in settling the building brief and in resolving the inevitable construction difficulties whenever and immediately they arise.

With this participation it will be feasible to practise continuous value engineering and to balance considerations of reliability, maintenance and running costs, against the initial capital costs in a manner consistent with the client's building performance specification. Crucial to this is the role of the cost consultant in both monitoring and influencing the commercial appraisals and the decisions of the members.

In any method of procuring buildings there are many links in the chain of communication and responsibility between the client and the building operative.

Each link is a potential break which under the new concept can be effectively ameliorated by positive management at the responsibility of the company.

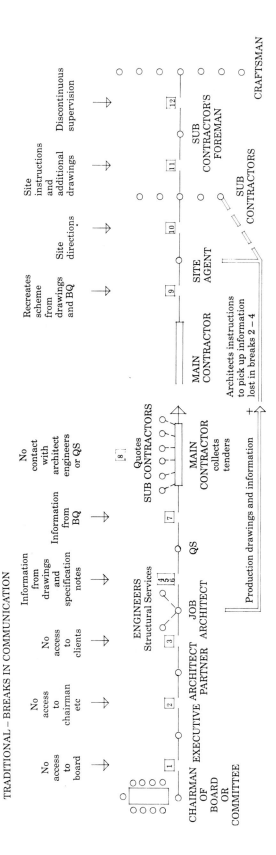

Figure A1.9 *Breaks in communication and areas of responsibility.*

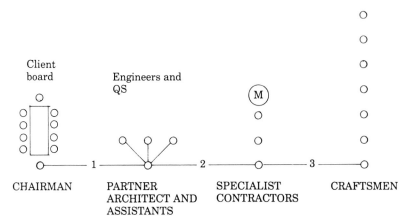

Figure A1.10 *Minimal breaks in communication and areas of responsibility.*

Price development from 'Target' towards 'Fixed-Price'

Where there is an evolving brief, an economic firm price deal can rarely be struck at the outset. Consequently, a series of stages is envisaged, at any of which the client can elect to hand over the financial responsibilities for the remainder of the development and the construction of the project, or indeed to abandon it.

Whilst there would be a preferred route to achieving a commitment on behalf of the client, the flexibility would exist to achieve this at an earlier stage if the client required it. One way to accommodate this would be by a target cost contract with a limit put on the client's financial exposure.

From the inception of the scheme, a cost plan is brought up to date at regular intervals and especially when significant changes are required. In normal circumstances, once a sufficient proportion of the work has been designed and priced (such proportion might vary from project to project), the scheme moves out of the development phase – in which the client incurs an increasing liability for the cost of that development work – through to the final gate when a lump sum for the whole project is submitted and accepted.

If the client wishes to have maximum certainty but minimum price, he may be advised to delay this passing over of financial responsibility until the design is completed and competitive tenders are available. But if, as is more likely to be the case, he wishes to achieve a level of price commitment at an earlier stage, a limit on price exposure can be fixed. Arrangements can then be made whereby the rules for ultimately determining the price to be paid can be established and whereby the client perhaps stands to share in a proportion of any savings achieved by the company below this limit.

At each stage cost, standards and quality are further defined. Thus the client early on has not only the choice of ensuring his commitment but also being able to rely on the best standards to be achieved within that price limit. Alternatively he can achieve precise standards to a given price and time-saving. In any event the speeding of the building programme will bring its own savings.

High quality, low cost and short time are the objectives of every client. These three objectives have to be kept in balance.

How they relate to one another is a basic matter which must be frankly and clearly addressed by the team and the client together. A formula for sharing profit or loss may be a useful remedial tool when the balancing act becomes unsteady.

The value of time and the programme

Traditional building processes are sequential and can be confrontational. By working together from the very outset of the building process it is possible to reduce the time period for the various stages by overlapping normally separate building stages and, by working as an integrated building team, avoid the waste of time and energy customary on the building site. Tasks that are not needed can be designed out, and the work can be rationalized into larger and less interdependent units. Design phases will incorporate the disciplines of construction technique and procurement realities, and construction ruled by insistence on quality and control. In the end it is all down to the quality and experience of people at every level.

The client will be urged to approve the start of development phases well in advance as compared with typical contract methods, and it is believed this new concept will give him confidence to do so. The lost periods of building time when the project is being considered by others (planning approval, building regulations approval, tendering, etc.) can also be fully utilized under this approach, so as to progress the building process.

At each of the break points in the reduced building programme (such as planning approval, staff on site, building regulations approval, all construction packages let, etc.) the client will have the option to negotiate a price which includes less for contingencies, as the risk is progressively reduced.

Flexibility is essential, so that both the constitution of the company

Figure A1.11 *The balance of time, quality and cost.*

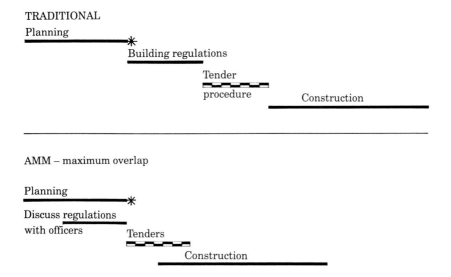

TRADITIONAL

Planning

Building regulations

Tender
procedure

Construction

AMM – maximum overlap

Planning

Discuss regulations
with officers

Tenders

Construction

Figure A1.12 *Potential time saving.*

and its commercial arrangements with the client may be tailored to achieve an alignment of interests in the particular circumstances of the project concerned. Open and in-depth discussion is therefore a vital first stage to this approach if all the advantages and opportunities are to be realized.

This new concept opens the door for leading professional and construction organizations to come together at the top to offer partnership to clients in the positive process of designing and constructing or renovating buildings in a direct and non-adversarial way.

Appendix 2
AMM/DPC Analysed

The following paper was prepared by Moxley Jenner and Partners at the request of the Department of the Environment.

It first briefly explains the background of AMM. The following pages of columnar material follows Dr Edward De Bono's method:

1 Stating a problem
2 Stating the negative aspects
3 Stating positive proposals
4 Stating a practical method

This of course does not mean to say that every architect, builder, trade contractor, surveyor, etc. suffers from all the disabilities listed in column 2. But in order to produce positive solutions to the effects which exist, it is necessary to examine the 'down-side' in order to see the way forward.

A review of AMM/DPC (Advanced Methods of Management/Direct Professional Control)

Terms

'AMM', – Advanced Methods of Management – is the generic term used by the Society for Advanced Methods of Management to describe attempts to rationalize and improve the management of the building process.

SAMM uses 'DPC' – Direct Professional Control – to describe one particular group of methods where a professional team provides a fiduciary (unbiased) service to the building owner, particularly in the co-ordination of separate trades contracts.

Concepts

AMM/DPC is not one concept, nor a chain of related techniques, but rather it is a radical review of the ills of the present building industry which suggest a series of reforms in many different areas in the following categories:

Communication, concentration, contract, professional training, professional practice, contractors' organization, quality control, cost control, speed of preparation and construction, delays, and the fragmentation of the professions.

Polarity

It is not a difficult task to identify most of the negative attitudes as exhibited within the professions and the building industry. Most of these attitudes have been generated by a desire to escape final responsibility in the case of error or failure. It is demonstrably difficult for a building owner to find out just who is at fault when mistakes are made. By no means all the participants in the building industry exhibit all of the negative aspects listed in the following schedule. But a sufficient number of them exhibit a sufficient proportion of negative attitudes to render the average performance of the British building industry down to a low level, as compared with American and German practice. It has recently been said that it is possible to build in America for dollars, what in this country it would cost in pounds and in half the time.

So what is required is a regeneration of positive attitudes and a desire to accept responsibility for actions rather than to escape from them.

Reinvention of the wheel

This restatement of positive attitudes and solutions to problems is not original. Broadly speaking the methods advocated are those which were common-place in the great days of renaissance building in this country, in France and in Italy. They are now growing in popularity in the USA, where CM now commands more than 30% of the market, and in Germany it is commonly practised in the building industry. Firms in this country often report remarkable results in terms of quality, cost and time, and one finds, on inspection, some of the techniques they have tried are those common to AMM/DPC. However, they have not before, as far as one knows, been brought together as a body of methods anᴜ values, then tried in practice on a fair number of jobs and found to produce the results claimed.

Approach

Generally, no two jobs are the same and the approach has to be designed to suit the particular job. However, the following is the backbone of all AMM/DPC jobs:

Not one collective tender but several, from carefully selected trade contractors.

A fully engaged professional team undertakes the work of co-ordinating the trade contractors.

The client (building owner) relies upon the architect's skill as co-ordinator, and the quantity surveyor's cost plan, rather than the main contractor's bid and the following JCT Contract. The latter is unreliable in terms of final cost and in estimated constructional time.

The professional forces are concentrated upon the job at high level.

There is direct two-way communication between the expert trade contractors, who actually do the building work, and the design team, who see the job right through from start to finish.

The professional team and the trade contractor

Why is it that architects and their professional colleagues, who choose this way of working, are reasonably successful at the management and co-ordination of trade contracts? There is in fact, a long tradition of this which now exists in the form of nominated or named sub-contract. This is where the architect feels that a particular group of trades are sufficiently important to insist that particular firms with those skills, are reserved to undertake the work, and that these matters are not left to the uncontrolled choice of the main contractor's buying department.

Summary

In return for relying on the architect, his professional colleagues, including the QS, and their professional skills in the selecting and managing of the trade contractors, the client gains considerable time saving, more consistent quality, and a better control of cost.

Categories	Negative aspects of existing situation	Positive theoretical basis for Direct Professional Control	Technique used in Direct Professional Control
1.00 COMMUNICATION			
1.01 Line: employer to craftsman	12 breaks or attenuations plus references back	Reduction to 2 or 3 breaks – reduces attenuation	Eliminate middlemen and deal directly with trade contractors.
1.02 Briefing: client to architect and team	Interposition of building programme executive and 'hierarchs' over job architect.	Direct and symbiotic meeting of minds.	Job architect at partner level, having experience and a good track record, in direct relationship with the client.
.1.03 Command (a)	Client loses control at contract stage. Economic modifications not possible. Any economic benefits from improvements flow to contractor.	Maximum fiduciary service to client.	Improvements and modifications positively accommodated until the trade contract cut-off dates, subject to overall programme economy.
(b)	Message confused by divided responsibilities and instructions.	Maintain control of scheme and cost.	Single line command and feedback from client to architect essential.
1.04 Drawings	Not readily understood, e.g. by craftsmen, too many codes, etc.	Drawings prepared with the type of recipient in mind for maximum comprehension.	Composite details with inter-relationshps shown and clear notes in understandable terms.

	Good basic set of drawings (in English) and site presence of designer. Synergistic interaction.	Good craftsmen capable of interpretation of intention from sound, basic set of drawings, allows feed-back and creative participation.	Too many drawings, academic dissociation from the construction process. No willingness to carry out work 'to the general intent of the basic architect's drawings'
	Sufficient on-site resources in terms of architects, engineers and their assistants, direct contact so that real needs can be identified and vexatious requests eliminated.	Clear issuing programme agreed at outset.	Drawings delivered too late, inadequate, without a clear programme.
1.05 Specification	Prepared by architect. The specification is often incorporated in the SECT and Report.	Clear written account of benefit to client, quantity surveyor and to the trade estimators and craftsmen.	Absent or inadequate.
1.06 SMM 6/7	SECT in straight forward terms in grouped items with times for each item.	Trade estimators and contractors must have the clearest understanding of	Not understood by craftsmen, client and some architects.

Categories	Negative aspects of existing situation	Positive theoretical basis for Direct Professional Control	Technique used in Direct Professional Control
		pricing information so that the right level of performance is provided and supervised.	
	Not written in the commonly used terms employed by trade contractors.	Foremen and craftsmen need to be selected for the appropriate standards required for each particular job.	Tender and negotiation clarifies standards required.
	No labour times furnished.	Programme information is essential.	Labour loading graph and sufficient staffing up of critical items.
1.07 Personal communication	Adversary site meetings.	In the absence of the claims-game all attitudes can become constructive.	On-site presence of compatible professional team.
	Poor team selection by dictat, leading to incompatibilities.	Team mutually selected, no large groups.	Negative members in any executive position, professional or trade,

			removed instanta. Key trade contractors' offices on-site next to professional team. Daily tour.
1.08 Correspondence, AIs, VOs, Minutes	Can be tinged with overtones of contract traps. AIs, VOs and Minutes often overlap and lead to a confusion between triggers for action, records for post mortem legal protection, and cost record information.	Site meeting minutes are the agreed record of action proposed, improvements and modifications agreed and establish co-ordination of trades. The meetings occur weekly and are at high level.	Site meeting minutes by architect/engineer are issued same day or very next day. Sent first class post to all affected by contract whether present at site meeting or not. An additional set may be cannibalized and analysed by subject headings to give continuous story for each trade or other item which appears regularly week by week.
2.00 CONCENTRATION 2.01 Geographical	Offices of the client, each firm in the professions, each trade contractor and the main contractor, and the site, are all in entirely different places in a region.	Bring together the senior professionals, site agent, contract's directors/ managers to the site office fully manned.	Conditions of tendering demands full-time site presence of senior management/directors in the key trades with necessary staff back-up.

Categories	Negative aspects of existing situation	Positive theoretical basis for Direct Professional Control	Technique used in Direct Professional Control
	Response time to problems therefore in weeks or months.	Response time in minutes or hours.	Experienced co-operative site agent employed by architect and works under his direction.
2.02 Individual	Typical senior architect may have responsibility for 20 or more jobs in various stages at any one time. Impossible to give predictive attention consistently to all of them (or any). Much of his time is therefore devoted to 'fire brigade' actions.	Senior professional people recruited or attached for length of project engagement. They thus are without other jobs to distract their concentration. Full-time appointments. Good renumeration.	Architects or associates are recruited on a job by job basis from firms able to take the necessary delegation. Thorough back-ground investigation. The commission depends upon the guarantee of time on site. Such people must be experienced, extrovert, capable, and have a good verifiable record. These people provide the nucleus of the site teams. Other professions are engaged at a complementary level.

3.00 CONTRACT
3.01 JCT and Others

Client until recently not represented on the drafting body of the JCT except by co-professionals. The contractors, in contra-distinction, and, unlike the other professionals, have their financial interest very much at heart. Contracts have become more elaborate and much of the risk has become laid at the client's door. However the client is generally the least experienced at such risk-taking. Elaborate management procedures (JCT Part II). Not comprehensible by most clients, many builders or professional men. Divides the client/professional team from the trade (works) contractors who actually build the building.

Simple forms that offer clear, priceable risks in encompassable amounts.

Contract leters with trade contractors of sound reputation. For bigger jobs, refer to the ACA Contract.
Separate trades contracts between the client and each trade contractor. Best buys from careful short-listed trade contractors. Negotiation is used where a unique service is offered. Negotiation on times and labour forces is essential to deal with critical paths in programmes.

Categories	Negative aspects of existing situation	Positive theoretical basis for Direct Professional Control	Technique used in Direct Professional Control
	Inhibits feedback from craftsman to designer. Design and construction artificially divorced.	Daily site presence and positive relationship with masters of trades. Most craft processes have a design content.	Site meetings held weekly. They formalize good relationships with senior firms' men. Daily contact with craftsmen and trade foremen encourages their positive contribution to the work. Morale improves and care, by craftsmen, markedly improves. This is a most important feature of quality performance, cf. BRE Report by M. Bentley.
4.00 PROFESSIONAL TRAINING			
4.01 Architects	Little or no site management training. Ethos fosters unnatural separateness of design and construction. Some instructors have had no real	Students respond readily to positive ideas and press for more information and opportunities for experience.	Positively advantageous to have at least one student on site during an AMM contract so that bit by bit a cadre of such experienced people is built up. Some

			Techniques:
	experience of the profession or industry.	universities are now setting exam questions in Part III on AMM/DPC. A number of universities and polytechnics are members of the Society for Alternative Methods of Management. A number of architectural practices are carrying out AMM with some degree of relish.	BSQI SECT Labour loading graphs Site co-operation
4.02 Quantity Surveyors	Few full time courses. Detailed view may obscure broad cost planning appreciation. Dedication to methods often are held at the expense of general needs.	Partner QSs can be excellent at cost control, and provide a positive input to such processes.	
5.00 PROFESSIONAL PRACTICE 5.01 Isolation	Isolation from the construction process through the malign influence of contract and a general desire to avoid too much responsibility.	Total involvement needed preferably where the action is.	Full-time, high calibre on-site team established as soon as possible – 'within the sound of the pile drivers' – concentrates minds.

Categories	Negative aspects of existing situation	Positive theoretical basis for Direct Professional Control	Technique used in Direct Professional Control
5.02 Practical involvement needed	Academic bias resulting from the Oxford Conference, and the establishment of a large number of Schools of Architecture in Universities has divorced architects from sites, and to some extent from public reaction.	Confidence is regained by active participation and learning from real situations. Need for formal courses in AMM/DPC. There is a need for models and prototyping.	Trades are pleased to furnish alternative samples and mock-ups.
5.03 Reality is three-dimensional	All communication now has to be forced through linear (words) or 2D (drawings) modulators in an attempt to describe 3D artifacts.		
5.04 Feedback	Little or no feed-back from craftsmen except where trade contractors have been 'nominated' or 'named'. There is now considerable pressure from the industry to reduce or eliminate nominations. Separate	No drawing-board hack can imagine all the skills and machines that are available in the specialist trade contractor's environment.	The weekly site meetings with trade contractors, particularly with their senior staff, together wth the daily contact on site with foremen and craftsmen, ensures the maximum feedback. If, as

we recommend, appropriate sections of the later stage of drawing and detailing is left until work starts on site on the early stages, there is a much greater opportunity for the detailed design work to be influenced by the specialist trade contractors and their craftsmen. The artificial isolation of these two interactive processes can therefore be, to some extent, unified as in the great renaissance days of architecture.

meetings are often held, for instance, – the contractor has his meeting with sub-contractors on one day and with the professional team on another day. This prevents productive interaction between the designers and the trade contractors. This thwarts the interest of the designer in construction management. Modifications and improvements suggested by trade contractors rarely find their way back to the benefit of the architect and his client.

Contract Management can be done by greater concentration at a higher level. A full-time professional team with an experienced site agent working with them is bound to be better than a

6.00 CONTRACTOR'S ORGANIZATION

6.01 Structure

Many medium and larger firms are now 'holding companies' with subsidiaries, each covering what used to be the original firm's specialist departments, e.g. joiners, plasterers, etc. together

Categories	Negative aspects of existing situation	Positive theoretical basis for Direct Professional Control	Technique used in Direct Professional Control
	with a contracts management department. Each company quotes in competition. Each contract won is completely sub-let down to and including the tea making. Main contractors are thus contracts managers, – more efficient in the short term.	contractor's site agent (commonly) running two or more sites.	Tender action and subsequent negotiations (on times) of each of the groups of trade contractors is the practical method. Carefully selected short-lists are required and prompt payment of accounts is undertaken, – cash flow, nowadays, being a major consideration.
6.02 (a) Buying department (b) Claims department (c) Management department	The Main Contractor's subsidiary contracting company usually has several departments – (a) a buying department, and (b) a claims department, and (c) a management department. The object of the buying department is to obtain the cheapest tenders with subcontractors and suppliers that the regime of SMM 6/7 and architect site	By going direct to the trades contractors, opportunities for reducing standards to the minimum tolerable is therefore reduced, because each of the individual areas of operation are smaller and more visible. Once the trade contractor realizes that he will be paid (quickly) for what he does, his claims attitude	

	inspections will allow. The object of the claims department is to maximize the claims potential that the drawings, documents, the architect's involvement and that the operation of the trades contractors presents.	diminishes and his willingness to co-operate increases.	Employ a good site agent to work on site with the architect's team and with any needed back-up staff.
(c) Management department	The main contractor fields a site agent charged with conflicting roles of co-ordinating subcontractors and maximizing claims. A site agent may have to look after more than one site at a time.	Make the co-ordination of trades part of the fiduciary service. Think of construction when designing. Carry through on site.	
6.03 Public Relations	Directors or senior men in the main contractor's organization often engage in developing contracts and persuading clients to use a package deal. When contracts are signed, new teams of hard men take over with different objectives, who do not always see the point of many of the early decisions.	It is beneficial if the same professional partner level people see the job through from brief to completion, understand the rationale of the design and details, and thus interpret the scheme on site with little or no fuss.	The ideal form is that where the professional partner or chief officer who helps to set up the brief sees the job through in all its stages, including construction on site, being directly involved, not just in a supervisory capacity.

Categories	Negative aspects of existing situation	Positive theoretical basis for Direct Professional Control	Technique used in Direct Professional Control
6.04 Contract Management and Trade Contractors	The evolution of the present main contracting system has taken only a couple of decades and it is better for the holding company from a profits point of view. It is not so effective in building up good will in the long term as the traditional forms. The present form, therefore, where the contractor merely manages trade contractors is not so good for the client or his professional advisers.	The crystallization of the builder's outfit into separate companies opens the way to others to take over the role of contract co-ordination. The field now has management consultants, in-house departments of large companies, QSs specializing in management, management contractors (like Bovis) CM in America, the German building contract system, Research into Site Management – RSM and AMM/DPC. It is thus a matter of devising the best system in the client's interest.	Unless the client has a fund of experience in procuring work from the building industry, he needs good unbiased advice from competent professionals. Thus many experienced clients continue to employ independent professional advice.

6.05 Management Consultants, etc.	There is a half-way house where a management consultant is introduced at contract stage. He has to learn the architect's and engineer's scheme from scratch and cannot therefore be aware in great detail of the rationale behind all the briefing and design decisions. He constitutes another element in the communication chain and increases the risk of incompatibilities occurring through adding to the numbers in the site information production and management teams.	Better to go for architects or engineers who are fully involved and aware of the principles and the details behind all the design decisions and who are interested and capable of site management.	Choose experienced professionals who are keen on site management and want to be involved in the making of buildings as a natural extension of the design and production drawing process.
6.06 Quality Control, morale & co-operation	The professional role in site supervision by the occasional visit becomes a policing job, but without the necessary contacts with the real constructors, i.e. the trade (works) contractors. So the professional is	Morale of site is re-orientated towards doing a good job and getting more work to follow.	Site meetings bring out into the open any potential lack of care that may be taking place between the trade contractors. Rational, good humoured examination most often generates positive and co-

Categories	Negative aspects of existing situation	Positive theoretical basis for Direct Professional Control	Technique used in Direct Professional Control
	emasculated and the trade contractors and others develop a tendency to get away with as much as possible.		operative procedures and attitudes.
6.07 Quality & Care	BRE report (1980) by Mike Bentley shows that failure to achieve quality is due to lack of care (85%) rather than lack of skill. Lack of care is due to lack of motivation to see the job as a whole, and a lack of concerned supervision.	Daily contact with professional team ensures plenty of interest and overseeing. Care and quality thus increase.	Develop for operatives a task cycle regime of 'brief: inspect (and rectify) : support : pass (and commend) : brief next task'. Task cycle should be optimum length (3 days to two weeks), or boredom sets in – (only applies to certain types of trade). Daily 'task and finish' is too short and is generally exploited.
7.00 COST CONTROL 7.01 Integration,	Though bills of quantities and SMM 6's (et seq) give a basis for equal tendering,	Write tender documents in terms familiar to the ordinary trade estimators,	BSQI and SECT with Report including drawings, brings the client

clarity and responsibility	they do not conveniently stretch to materials and labour programming and ordering in their present forms. Some trades make their own estimation of standards required, – in different terms. Trade estimators rarely see full details and drawings of the work for which they are tendering. Except when nominated, (nomination is discouraged by the industry's establishment), directors and estimators do not meet to discuss improvements and potentials with architects and engineers at tendering stage.	integrate absolutely with drawings and spec. descriptions. Encourage contact with designers before and during tendering process so that the client can get full advantage in improvements and potentials.	in immediate touch with the fine tuning of the brief in terms of cost and level of provision. Tender lists for each trade must be vetted by references, inspections and personal enquiry. Selected trade contractors must be able to meet the programme and be willing to augment their forces if on the critical path. Must be willing to accept duplication and determination clauses added to the contract. Certificates fortnightly or monthly. Final certificates within 2 months.
8.00 SPEED OF PREPARATION AND CONSTRUCTION	The worst case is where each stage is taken end to end, – so that there are no	With the client's knowledge and approval, once the scheme design is	Erect a programme of realistic cut-off dates for client information on

Categories	Negative aspects of existing situation	Positive theoretical basis for Direct Professional Control	Technique used in Direct Professional Control
8.01 Parallel working & the value of time	overlaps. This protects those in charge of each stage from the risk of making wrong assumptions, but it takes unnecessarily long. Time is valuable. Calculate the value of days/weeks/ months saved to the client or occupants, and use this information against which improvements can be measured.	approved, much of the ensuing work can be overlapped and with benefit. Structural and services design and detail production work can run in parallel. Planning approval can, on occasions, be overlapped. Building regulations approval should not delay the process for a competent professional team can follow regulations except where interpretation becomes a problem. Consultation with officials is necessary. The design of office partitions, fittings and furniture, suspended ceilings, etc., can take place during construction period.	following trades to allow for final design, tendering and mobilization. The QS allows tranches of money for these sections of the works to which tenderers comply. On site team tackles the work in the sequence of the cut-off programme. The client, therefore, has more time to develop new processes, machinery, etc., to suit the emerging enterprise, and develops a better understanding of the architecture sooner.

8.02 Available work interfaces	Random inspection of most building sites invariably shows many areas (interfaces) where work could (reasonably) be going on. 2D programmes do not comprehensibly show up these interfaces.

(e.g. What percentage of erected scaffolding is in proper and economic use on the average site?) | It takes the 3D trained imagination of the architect to recognize these potentials. Any task which is three weeks or more in length can be staffed up economically. | The on-site presence of the professional team ensures that the available work interfaces are fully employed. |
| 8.03 Programming | Bar charts are useful but limited. CPNs are too elaborate and have far too many events for ordinary comprehension. They do not readily show time progression. | Programmes must be obvious and clear to all the participants and easily updateable. | Labour loading graphs and 25-event CPN sketches on a time base can illustrate relationships and critical paths on a macro, medium, or micro focus. Keep information stations round site updated with local programmes. Keep groups in touch with relevant programme information. |

Categories	Negative aspects of existing situation	Positive theoretical basis for Direct Professional Control	Technique used in Direct Professional Control
8.04 Time-keeping	Sloppiness about starting, finishing and breaks.	Any of the workforce in work areas should be working.	Agree time keeping in advance. If possible, have the catering subcontractor operating on site, with a daily use programme.
9.00 DELAYS 9.01 Strikes	Sites employing much over 120 men are more prone to strikes.	Good trade contractors will not take on unknown men.	Contracts should be conditional upon not taking on unknown men, or at least taking great care to operate early dismissal provisions if in doubt.
9.02 Materials shortages	Material or equipment specified may be in short supply.	See if specification can be modified to use available material.	Organize 'seek, find, collect and deliver' service for critical items. Check cost against value of time saved and agree with client.
9.03 Poor trade co-ordination	Can be used by the agent as a way of increasing claims for extras. The general	Ensure that predictive co-ordination of trades works in the client's best interest.	Site meetings quickly demonstrate where improvements are

	maximizing of difficulties is often a part of the claims technique.	Full time professional site involvement exposes attempts to orchestrate such possibilities.	possible. Trade contractors who will not comply are duplicated or terminated quickly, (infrequent in practice)
9.04 Extensions of time	A BRE report referred to average over-runs in the order of 30% with the implied extra costs of about 19% as *average*. In spite of this, clients and authorities continue to use and to recommend the same orthodox procedures.	AMM/DPC improves time and controls cost more closely, (ref. BRE report – PD 87/77).	Closer control as before described.
10.00 FRAGMEN-TATION OF THE PROFESSIONS	Architects, QSs, structural engineers, services engineers, project managers, landscape architects, planners, surveyors, package deal builders, etc., all have overlapping functions. The	There is a need for the reintegration of any of these functions to provide greater coherence.	Select professional teams by mutual process for competence, experience and compatibility. Not too many in each team, (6 maximum) and keep a firm eye on the developing positive attitudes. Remove

Categories	Negative aspects of existing situation	Positive theoretical basis for Direct Professional Control	Technique used in Direct Professional Control
	client is confused by all these roles.		negative people immediately in their own, and the client's interest.
11.00 COSTS & FEES	Main contractor's head office overheads (offices, cars, head office staff, etc.) and his profit, amount to (currently) 11½% – (in normal times) (DHSS), of the contract sum, (can be more).	Make direct use of the trade contractor system and save the main contractor's overheads and profit.	Professional teams are paid normal fees for normal service. The rapidity of the job finances the bigger concentration of higher-grade professional people. A fee is charged for site management by the professional design – construction team through the lead consultant.

Appendix 3

A typical agenda for an AMM site meeting

An example from current practice of a typical agenda for an AMM site meeting. This includes items of the management of preliminaries which would not normally occur at a conventional site meeting for an orthodox contract.

SOUTH BANK TECHNOPARK
Site Meeting No: 14
Date : Tuesday 30th April 1985   Venue : Polytechnic Building,
London Road, Room 261.

Time : 10.00 a.m.

AGENDA

1.1 *Minutes of last*
     Site Meeting

1.2 *Project Manager's*
     Report

     A. *Project Manager's*
         Meetings

         (1) Summary of
              Meetings

(2) Matters Arising

B. *Instructions to Date*

C. *Construction Programme*

(1) Review & Comments

(2) Progress

(3) Forecast

(4) Other Programmes

(5) Other Matters

D. *Statutory Undertakings*

E. *Industrial Relations*

F. *Trade Contractor's Observations*

1.3 *Architect's Report*

A. Local Authorities

B. Client

C. Occupant

D. Information

1.4 *Structural Engineer's Report*

A. Co-ordination & Progress

B. Information

1.5 *Building Services*
    Consultant's Report

    A. Co-ordination &
       Progress

    B. Information

    C. *Main Trades*

        (1) Brickwork

        (2) a) Windows
            b) Conservatories
            c) Staircases

        (3) a) Mechanical
            b) Plumbing
            c) Electrical
               Services

            d) Security
            e) Telephones

        (4) Roofing

        (5) Groundworks/
            Landscaping

        (6) Carpentry/Joinery

        (7) Fire Shutters

        (8) Plastering

        (9) Decorations

        (10) Lifts

        (11) Balustrades

        (12) Suspended Ceilings

        (13) Floor Finishes

1.6 *Quantity Surveyor's*
    Report

      A. Valuations

      B. Forecast

1.7 *Safety & Welfare*

      A. Site Security

      B. Safety Standards,
         Accidents, First Aid

      C. Site Accommodation
         & Storage

      D. Temporary Services

1.8 *Any Other Business*

1.9 *Date & Venue of*
    Next Meeting

Appendix 4
Typical drawing issue record

The following is just one page of a typical set of drawing issue records tabled at site meetings to tell everyone of the new drawings and the amended existing drawings which are available to other consultants and trade contractors.

DRAWING ISSUE RECORD
SOUTH BANK TECHNOPARK

Issue Date
5.85

CONTRACT PREFIX: _719_   SOURCE: *CM ARCHITECTS & PLANNERS (MJP)*

SHEET _1_ OF _8_

TITLE	DRW. NO.	28.03.84	27.06.84	8.8.84	14.9.84	26.10.84	1.11.84	20.11.84	2.85	3.85	4.85
Location Plan	15										
Site Survey	22										
Site plan/details	50	—				A			B		C
Site Grading plan	51	—							A		B
Ground floor plan	AG	—			A	B				C	
Ground floor reflected ceiling plan	ARG				—		A			B	
Ground floor door plan	ADG							—	A	B	C
First floor plan	A1	—			A	B					
First floor reflected ceiling plan	AR1				—		A				
First floor door plan	AD1							—	A	B	
Second floor plan	A2	—			A	B				C	
Second floor reflected ceiling plan	AR2				—		A				
Second floor door plan	AD2							—	A	B	C
Roof/Plant room plan	A3	—		A							

RECIPIENTS	NO. OF COPIES					
Moxley, Jenner & Ptnrs – Site	28	15	20	25	20	20
Roughton & Fenton – London			2	2		
Roughton & Fenton – Site						
Voce & Case			6	2		
Sulzer Bros.			3	2		
Stitson White Services			1			
Lewis Electrical						
Sugrue Bros. – H.O.						
Sugrue Bros. – Site						
Irvine & Whitlock						
Greyrook						
Soamvale – H.O.			1			
Baileys Roofing						

Appendix 5
Typical work monitoring record

This is a typical example of a job monitor sheet which gives an assessment of the percentage completion of the various trades and other activities.

Those in charge of site operations are inclined to be rather optimistic about the degree of completion of a particular operation. It is remarkable how many jobs stay at 90% or 95% for so long!

DATE *26.4.85* *Monitor No. 20* **OPERATIONS** *Sheet 1 of 4*	BA			C			B		
	Grd.	1st	2nd	Grd.	1st	2nd	Grd.	1st	2nd
BRICKWORK									
External Brickwork	100	100	100	100	100	90	90	90	90
Corridor Blockwork	100	100	95	100	100	98	95	50	50
Unit Partitions Blockwork	98	100	98	100	100	90	30	30	30
Concrete Slabs – Fire Walls at Roof	✕	✕	90	✕	✕	50	✕	✕	Nil
Prepare Walls for Decorations	100	90	80	100	90	80	80	40	Nil
Brickwork to D.P.C.	100	✕	✕	100	✕	✕	100	✕	✕
Toilets	✕	✕	✕	100	90	95	✕	✕	✕
Lift Shafts	✕	✕	✕	100	100	75	90	Nil	Nil
Plantrooms	✕	✕	100	✕	✕	✕	✕	✕	✕
Fire Shutter Lintel etc.	100	100	80	100	100	90	100	50	50
WINDOWS									
Windows & Sealant	97	95	95	95	95	85	10	Nil	Nil
Curtain-Walling	=	Nil	=	✕	✕	✕	=	Nil	=
Conservatory Glazing	=	Nil	=	=	Nil	=	=	10	=
Internal Sealant	90	=	=	=	Nil	=			
ELECTRICAL									
Electrical Carcass/Wire – Units	100	100		100	95	=	Nil	=	
Lighting 2nd Fix – Units	98	90	=	=	Nil	=			
Power 2nd Fix – Units	95	90	Nil	20	25	=	Nil	=	
Electrical Carcass/Wire – Corridor	100	100	20	100	100	=	Nil	=	
Lighting 2nd Fix – Corridor	100	100	10	100	100	=	Nil	=	
Fire Alarm Carcass – Corridor	100	100	Nil	100	100	Nil	100	100	Nil
Fire Alarm 2nd Fix – Corridor	95	95	Nil	95	95	Nil			
Power 2nd Fix – Corridor	=	=	=	Nil	=	=			
External Lighting Carcass/2nd Fix	95/	95/	95/	95/	95/	95/	95/	95/	95/

DATE 26.4.85 Monitor No. 20 OPERATIONS Sheet 2 of 4	BA			C			B		
	Grd.	1st	2nd	Grd.	1st	2nd	Grd.	1st	2nd
ELECTRICAL – Contd.									
Electrical Carcass/Wire – Toilets	✕	✕	✕				✕	✕	
Electrical 2nd Fix – Toilets	✕	✕			Nil		✕	✕	
Plant Rooms	✕	✕	10	✕	✕	✕	✕	✕	
MECHANICAL									
Rads. & Final Connections – Units	97	97	97	90	90	85	85	85	85
Test Pipework – Units	100	100	100	100	100	100	100	100	100
Insulate Pipework – Units	100	100			Nil				
Mechanical Carcass – Corridors	100	100	90	100	100	100	100	100	100
Test Pipework – Corridors	100	100	80	100	100	100	100	100	100
Insulate Pipework – Corridors	100	100	✕	90	✕	✕	Nil		✕
Radiators – Corridors	90	50			Nil				
Hosereel Cabinets – Corridors	100				Nil				
Plant Room Installation	✕	✕	80	✕	✕	✕	✕	✕	
JOINERY									
Timber Grounds	95	95	90	90	90	90		Nil	
Window Board Fixings – Units	85	✕	✕	85	✕	✕	Nil	✕	✕
Window Boards – Units	85	✕	✕	85	✕	✕	Nil	✕	✕
Door Frames/Arch. – Units	85	60	10			Nil			
Doors, Locks, etc. – Units	85	Nil	5			Nil			
Door Furniture – Units	10				Nil				
Door Frames, Doors – Corridors					Nil				
Door Furniture – Corridors					Nil				

DATE 26.4.85 Monitor No. 20 OPERATIONS Sheet 3 of 4	BA			C			B		
	Grd.	1st	2nd	Grd.	1st	2nd	Grd.	1st	2nd
ROOFING									
Roof Soakers, etc.	X	X	100	X	X	100	X	X	100
Roof at Fire Walls	X	X	50	X	X	25	X	X	Nil
DECORATIONS									
Soffit Decorations – Units	98	98	X	50	60	X	15	15	X
Initial Wall Decorations – Units	100	90	Nil	80	50	Nil			
H.L. Decorations – Corridors	90	90	Nil	90	90				
Joinery Decorations	33				Nil				
Corridor Decorations					Nil				
Toilet Decorations	X	X	X		Nil		X	X	X
External Decs. to Balconies					Nil				
MISCELLANEOUS									
Fire Shutters – Corridors	100	50	Nil	100	100		Nil		
Corridor Plastering	98	90	Nil	85	65	Nil	5	Nil	
Telephone Block Wiring	80	80	X	80	80	X	80	80	X
Security Wiring/2nd Fix	100/Nil								
Fire-Stop Floors – Units	95	100		95	95		Nil		
Fire-Stop Walls – Units	100	100	Nil	100	50		Nil		
Bldrs. Work – Elecs. – Corridor	100	100	Nil	100	100		Nil		
Waste Stack Sleeves	100	X	100	100	X	100	100	X	100
M/G to Stack Sleeves	100	X	100	100	X	100	100	X	100
Clean out for Decorations	90	45	Nil	80	80		Nil		
Remove temporary lighting	90	90	Nil	90	90		Nil		
M/G Walls (Pipes, Cables, etc.)	98	50	80	95	90	30		Nil	
Waste Stack Cover Plates	Nil	X	Nil	X	Nil	X	Nil	X	Nil

DATE 26.4.85 Monitor No. 20 OPERATIONS Sheet 4 of 4	BA			C			B		
	Grd.	1st	2nd	Grd.	1st	2nd	Grd.	1st	2nd
SUSPENDED CEILINGS									
Suspended Ceilings – Corridors	75				Nil				
Suspended Ceilings – Units			Nil		Nil			Nil
FLOOR FINISHES									
Floor Finish – Corridors					Nil				
Floor Finish – Units			Nil		Nil			Nil

Appendix 6

The placing and management of building contracts

As an interesting tail note this is an extract from a 1944 document from the Central Council for Works and Buildings which states many principles about the organization and management of building contracts that are still true today.

The Placing and Management of Building Contracts

I rom the report of the Central Council For Works and Buildings, Ministry of Works. HMSO 1944.

Much depends on the building owner. His business is to choose a good architect, to keep in close touch with him, and to give him full opportunities of doing his work under the best conditions.

This is by no means always done. The average building owner waits a long time before deciding to put up a new building. Once he makes up his mind to do so he is impatient to receive sketch drawings and close estimates of cost. Often he thinks that the obtaining of tenders is the only way by which he can satisfy himself as to cost and he presses the architect and quantity surveyor to get the contract fixed. The contract price in these circumstances contains a large number of provisional items which may prove quite unreliable; but this does not dissuade the building owner from entering into a contract as he often thinks that the sooner the work can be commenced upon the site the sooner the job will be finished.

There could be no greater mistake. The result of a rushed job of this sort is that nobody has really thought out the details; the owner and the architect, neither of whom has had the opportunity of studying the plans in detail, frequently change their minds; all sorts of improvements, mistakes and difficulties are discovered as the job goes on. The architect is constantly forced to instruct the builder to make variations from the original contract, each one of which causes delay and extra cost, and gives rise to claims for additional payments by the builder.

Another result is that the contract is usually signed long before the details of the various sub-contracts have been settled, and indeed before the architect, who takes responsibility for selecting many of the sub-contractors, has even decided which firms he intends to nominate. The contractor, therefore, when he signs the contract, does not know when each sub-contractor will be ready to begin his job, what his needs will be nor how long it will take him to finish. No reliable time and progress schedule can be made and no effective planning of the work is possible.

In all cases it is of the utmost importance that full and detailed drawings, specifications, bills of quantities and estimates should be prepared before the main contract is let, and that subsequent alterations should be reduced to a minimum.

The owner should insist on the completion of detailed drawings and specifications by the architect and should himself do his thinking and make his final decisions on a careful study of these documents; he should not wait to see what the job looks like as it goes up and then change his mind or make new suggestions. The contract drawings and the bills of quantities should accurately represent the work which will ultimately be carried out.

When the owner wishes to insist on undue hurry, the architect should endeavour to convince him of the importance of having time to complete his designs in detail.

The builder should also be in a position to insist on full particulars before starting work, but he is often not listened to, and indeed, even though the inadequately detailed job will cost more, the builder can usually get claims for extras.

The responsibility for this rush and inefficiency lies squarely on the shoulders of the building owner. He can prevent it if he wishes. He thinks he is going to get a cheaper and quicker job by rush methods, but he is profoundly mistaken. The work will take longer and cost more and he is the chief sufferer.

One of the major reforms in the building industry, therefore, is the education of the building owner to adopt businesslike methods in the preliminaries of the contract.

Bibliography

ACA (Association of Consultant Architects) Contract, Second Edition (Obtainable from RIBA Bookshop, 66 Portland Place, W1N 4AD).

ACA Illustrated Dictionary of Architects (Obtainable from ACA, Buchanan's Wharf, Redcliffe Books, Bristol BS1 6HT. *Tel.* 0272 256 006).

Bentley, M. J. C. (1981) 'Quality Control on Building Sites'. B.R.E. Report.

Emett, Patrick, FRICS (Wrightson, Pitt & Emett. *Tel.* 0272 266 461).

Heller, R. *The Business of Winning* (Sidgwick & Jackson).

HMSO (1944) 'The placing and management of building contracts'. Report of the Central Council for Works and Buildings, Ministry of Works.

Moxley, R. (1984) *An Architect's Guide to Fee Negotiations* (Architecture and Building Practice Guides, Architectural Press).

RIBA Clients Advisory Service, 66 Portland Place, W1N 4AD.

RIBA, *The Drawings Collections* (Obtainable from RIBA, 1 Portman Square, London W1).

Spring, Martin (1984) 'Managed by Architects' in *Building 2*, 2nd November, p. 40.

Weiss, W. (1979) 'The Architectural Practice, Organisation and Structure of the Construction Industry in West Germany' in *The Society for the Advancement of Methods and Management Newsletter*, No. 5, July.

Index